Sexual Identity

SEXUAL IDENTITY

Sex Roles and Social Change

BETTY YORBURG

A WILEY-INTERSCIENCE PUBLICATION

JOHN WILEY & SONS, New York · London · Sydney · Toronto

Library of Congress Cataloging in Publication Data:

Yorburg, Betty.
    Sexual identity; sex roles and social change.

    "A Wiley-Interscience publication."
    1. Sex role.   2. Identity.   3. Personality and culture.   I. Title.

BF692.Y67   301.41   73-14905

ISBN 0-471-97810-8

Printed in the United States of America

10 9 8 7 6 5 4 3 2

To Harriet and Bob

PREFACE

Male and female are biological categories; masculinity and femininity are social definitions. Conceptions of ideal masculine and feminine behavior and emotions are taught to individuals beginning very early in life. These conceptions are transmitted through the roles that people learn in their status as males or females. And in any particular society, at any particular time, these learned, sex-typed role definitions and expectations typically result in differing basic self images, or sexual identities for men and for women.

Males and females have always had somewhat different self images or identities. But definitions of ideal feminine and masculine traits and behavior have varied in different societies, and in the same society at different times. There is hardly a single emotion, ability, or activity that has not been defined as masculine, feminine, or both, in one society or another, at one time or another.

Why, then, have ideals of masculinity and femininity, and resulting sexual identities, varied in human societies? Why are there few distinctions between the sexes in some societies? Why are there many and strong distinctions in other societies? To what extent are sex-typed role distinctions biologically inevitable? Finally, how can we explain the variations in the authority relationships between the sexes, which have occurred throughout human history?

These are the questions I will answer here, drawing on factual information from biology, anthropology, history, psychology, and sociology. We badly need an accurate, up-to-date, comprehensive approach to the topic of sexual identity, including how and why this factor has varied historically. If we are not predestined by biology to think, act, and feel in certain *specific* ways (and I do not think we are), we must be fully aware of the choices open to us. We must understand the costs and the consequences of the choices that we make, and we must be aware of the extent to which these costs and consequences are inevitable.

Developments in science and technology, rapid social change, and the women's movement are currently providing the motivation for questioning traditional sex-typed role definitions. Increasingly, men and women can base decisions about their activities, identities, and destinies on knowledge rather than on dogma or tradition. The behavioral sciences can provide this knowledge and insight.

This is a major challenge to contemporary science—at least as crucial as the concern with runaway technology, environmental destruction, the troubled nuclear family, racial conflict, and the inevitability of human aggression. Conceptions of sexual identity are the core of human identity, and, ultimately of human relationships. The races and classes have remained separate; the sexes have not and cannot remain separate. If we can cope with the question of how and why problems arise in the man–woman relationship, major areas of human experience—in politics, family life, and economic life—will benefit, I believe, and in very important ways.

BETTY YORBURG

The City College
of The City University of New York
New York, New York
September 1973

CONTENTS

Sexual Identity

1 | The Problem

Identity is the total conception that people have of who they are. It includes all the beliefs that make up the individual's conception of self. It also includes the beliefs that people have about their worth as human beings—beliefs that determine self confidence and self esteem.

Sexual identity is the image of the self as a male or a female and convictions about what membership in that group implies. Sexual identity, the individual's basic, sex-typed self image, is built up gradually from early infancy. It is the result of learned conceptions about the self, as a male or as a female. It includes beliefs about how one *ought* to think, act, and feel by virtue of having been born male or female. It includes learned ideals of masculine and feminine behavior and the proper authority relationships between the sexes.

Ideals of masculinity and femininity provide standards for judging emotions and behavior, privileges and limitations. These ideals result in evaluations of the self as good, bad, inferior, superior, desirable, or undesirable. If people in a society define beautiful as feminine and brilliant as masculine, a female who is brilliant and unattractive (unattractive by that society's standards) will feel unfeminine and undesirable.

If males in a society are defined as superior—physically, emotionally, or intellectually—this idea becomes part of the self

1

image of males and females. It affects the relative self confidence and self esteem of the sexes. It affects the goals that women and men will seek, and it affects the means that each group will choose to achieve these goals.

The ideals of masculinity and femininity that are learned by males and females, resulting in sex-typed identities, are usually held in common by many people in a society. They are passed down from generation to generation. They are part of the culture—the social heritage of values, knowledge, customs, and skills—that is transmitted to human beings in particular societies, beginning at the moment of birth. These conceptions are transmitted in the form of different expectations from females and from males in the performance of their respective roles.

If passivity and obedience are feminine ideals in a society, most little girls in that society will be taught and expected to be unassertive and obedient. And they will, typically, display these traits in their roles as daughter, student, employee, and wife. Each one will develop an identity in which she views herself as unaggressive and submissive. She will believe that females *ought* to be unaggressive and submissive. And if she is assertive and dominating she will feel guilty and unfeminine.

In some societies, the distinctions in the self images, personality traits, and behavior of the sexes are few and rather weak. This situation is reflected in language. The terms male and female exist in all languages; the terms masculine and feminine exist in societies in which strong distinctions are made between the expected behavior, temperaments, and abilities of the sexes.

The term identity is not found in all languages. It is a modern term that did not exist in most traditional societies, where identity was bestowed at birth, was seldom questioned, and was rarely changed. Peasants did not become kings. They could not even *imagine* themselves as kings.

The term identity did not exist because the notions it represents were not the source of problems. People rarely questioned or were confused about who or what they were. Nor did they separate themselves from their groups, as distinct personalities with individual needs and desires, to the extent that they do now. Men and women did not need concepts such as identity, self, self image, and self confidence. The group, not the self, was the basic unit of the society.

In rapidly changing, highly industrialized societies, however, identity tends to become vague, unstable, and debatable. Traditional ideals of masculinity and femininity, as these define sexual identity, become increasingly inappropriate—outmoded, contradictory, irrelevant, or detrimental to changing societal and individual needs. Social conditions change, but values and ideals often lag behind.

Identities become fragmented as individuals experience ambiguities and contradictions in their roles. Roles become less rigid and identities more flexible as alternative life styles multiply. Roles do not disappear in modern societies, but they tend to become more negotiable. Power and ethics become increasingly situational and less predetermined by culture. Roles, more often, are worked out on the basis of individual preference rather than societal dictate.

We cannot live without agreed-upon roles. Sooner or later, even anarchic groups develop roles—scripts or blueprints that guide the behavior of members of the group. We cannot have an orderly social life unless people know what to expect of one another in recurring social situations. We cannot survive unless people have relatively stable conceptions of their rights and obligations. These conceptions and expectations are somewhat less arbitrary and inflexible in industrial societies, particularly among urban, highly educated men and women, but they exist, nonetheless.

The trend toward greater freedom and experimentation in the roles people play is just beginning. In all societies, the majority of men and women are still committed to traditional, culturally defined, sex-typed roles. Thus it is still possible to speak of virtually universal ideals of masculinity and femininity, of sex-typed personality traits, of typical authority relationships between the sexes, and, consequently, of typical female and typical male self images or identities.

But now identity *can* be achieved, at least in part and by some people. Now some options are available in the ways men and women can act, think, and feel in major areas of life. It becomes important, then, to understand how sexual identities are learned and why they have varied for women and men—historically and at present. Given such understanding, we are better equipped to make changes. We can know better what is possible, what is necessary, what is arbitrary, and what is destructive in the relationships and identities of the sexes.

Unfortunately, we do not have adequate firsthand information about the step-by-step process by which the sexes build up their distinct identities (insofar as these are distinct, typically). This is especially true for past societies. There was relatively little interest in this topic until recently. Anthropologists, for example, rarely focused on this problem in studying societies that have since undergone great change.

We are just beginning to collect this kind of information about the sexes in contemporary societies. Much of our present data comes from reanalyses of child development studies—but the development of sex differences was not the original focus of these investigations. Only recently have psychologists been making careful observational studies, of mother–child relationships in particular, which indicate the very subtle ways in which different sex-typed expectations operate to affect differentially the personalities of very young female and male infants.

It is difficult to describe the varying identities of the sexes in human history. Identity must be inferred from the roles men and women have played. Role playing can be observed; identity cannot be observed—at least not directly. I think it is legitimate to make the inference, however, because for the most part we are what we do. Identity is the product of the roles individuals have played and the definitions of self contained in these roles. These definitions begin to affect identity from the moment the infant develops a sense of self as an acting and acted-upon being. And this occurs when infants can voluntarily and self consciously act—attempting to bring food to their mouths or touching their toes, for example. It occurs when they deliberately and knowingly respond to maternal gestures with a reciprocal gesture—a smile, for example. We know then that the infant has a sense of self as an acting and acted-upon being.

Because identity is not easily measured and observed, and because I am concentrating here mainly on the changing status and roles of the sexes historically, I have used quotations from contemporary autobiographical sources to illustrate, sometimes quite dramatically, the internal dimension of identity or self image as this varies, typically, in major areas of the world. These illustrations will serve to clarify the effects on identity of changing roles—of changing economic and educational opportunities, and of changing values—and the relationship between role and identity.

It may be that ideals of masculinity and femininity will some day disappear from human societies. Eventually, too, the terms masculinity and femininity may be eliminated from languages. Perhaps even the concept of sexual identity will disappear, to be replaced by the notion of human identity or individual identity. Perhaps sexual identity will, in the course of time, contain no notion of how people *ought* to behave and feel because they are biologically male or female.

These possibilities are discussed at the very end of my undertaking here—after I have traced and explained historical and present-day variations in the socially defined roles and resulting identities of women and men in major types of societies.

SCIENTIFIC APPROACHES.   Science is concerned with what *is* and only indirectly with what *ought* to be. Scientists are bound by observed facts. Their job is to explain the how and the why of the material and the nonmaterial universe, past and present. They deal with the physical and mental aspects of human existence, which can be objectively described, explained, and predicted.

Only in the past century, since the birth of the social sciences, have the typical differences in the personalities and behavior of men and women been studied scientifically, and this development has occurred largely within the past fifty years. Basic to most of these researches has been the question of the relative importance of biology and learning in determining the temperaments, aptitudes, and activities of women and men.

The major problem has been that the two sets of factors—biology and environment—cannot be separated. Environment begins to operate on the fetus at the moment of conception: culture and social circumstances affect what the mother eats, how much she works or rests, her health, her moods, her attitudes toward pregnancy, and the type and quality of prenatal care she receives (if, indeed, she receives any at all). While heredity and environment operate simultaneously and inseparably, however, we can try to evaluate the *relative* weight or importance of each set of factors in determining the varying roles, or scripts, that men and women have lived out in the recurring dramas of everyday life in various societies. To do this we need information from the biological sciences about the typical anatomical, chromosomal, and hormonal differences between the sexes. Since we also need to understand the importance of culture, learning, and experience for sexual identity, we look to the social sciences, particularly anthropology, history, psychology, and sociology.

History and anthropology give us data about natural experiments in the past life of human beings— situations in which there have been variations in one or more factors—the level of technological development, the economic role of women, the structure and functioning of the family, for example. We can then look at the identities, attitudes, values, and behavior of men and women under such varying conditions. If we find that strong variations in the personalities and relationships of men and women accompany certain kinds of social conditions and learning experiences, we can begin to assess the relative importance of environment in determining sexual identity.

This kind of information is essential because we cannot experiment with human beings as we can with nonhumans or with inanimate objects. Humans have rights, values, and feelings; stones and stars do not. The attitudes of subjects and experimenters can distort the results of experiments, as well as the interpretations of these results. Furthermore, humans inhabit highly complex environments that are impossible to duplicate in an experimental setting for the purpose of varying one or more factors artificially. Therefore, we look to natural variations in the environments men and women have lived in and to actual variations in their typical life experiences and behavior. If men, everywhere and at all times, have been more physically aggressive than women, we have convincing evidence that there is a strong genetic factor in male aggression. But if there is one exception, if there is even one society in which women, typically, have been more aggressive than men, we have evidence, then, that culture and learning can override whatever biological predispositions exist in men and women—at least with respect to aggression.

To understand specifically how and why environment, learning, and experience result in the development of typical personality traits in men and women, we turn to psychology and sociology. Psychologists focus on the effects of certain social relationships and experiences—authoritarian as opposed to permissive parent–child relationships, for example—on emotions, motivation, and thought. Sociologists have the same interest, but we add another dimension to the focus of the psychologist. We locate people socially. We place them in particular groups, classes, nations, generations, and occupations. We look for what is typical in the self images and personalities (particularly atti-

tudes, values, and beliefs) of people who are members of particular clubs, gangs, mental hospital wards, colleges, factories, and
communes. We determine, for example, whether permissive
parent–child relationships in certain societies are more typical
of the middle class or the working class, and why. We can then
understand certain typical differences in personality—in
achievement motivation, conformity, prejudice, or religiosity, for
example—between the two classes.

We look for the typical frustrations, gratifications, and conflicts of men and women in the nineteenth century or in the
twentieth century, in Japan or in the United States, among
black or white, and in those who are under thirty or over sixty-
five. We share the psychologists' interest in personality development and change, but we focus more on the effects of social location, in time, in place, and in various other social universes, as
this affects typical kinds of learning experiences and human
relationships.

A girl born into a black, poor, rural, American, southern family in the 1940s will have had certain life experiences typically
different from those of a male infant born into a white, rich,
urban, English family in the 1970s. Such locating factors as
class, nationality, generation, urban–rural residence, race, and
sex are different for the two infants. Their relationships with
their parents will be dissimilar, typically, as will their relationships with teachers, friends, siblings, employers, and strangers.
The roles that they learn in various social situations will differ.
And these dissimilarities will result in typically different identities, attitudes, values, and ways of handling emotion in the two
children—differences that will usually persist throughout their
lives.

Poll takers are usually sociologists who have been trained in
survey research methods. They measure rather superficial aspects of personality, namely, attitudes, as these are verbalized in
opinions. Opinion researchers are very careful to locate their re-

spondents in various social universes: by class, sex, age, religion, race, area of the country, and level of education. Usually opinions vary according to these locating factors—as do other aspects of personality.

The roles people play are differently defined in different cultures and subcultures. Roles differ in content according to where people are located in time and place. The role of wife is learned and played out very differently in the working class and in the upper class, for example. The concept of role is as central to sociology as the concept of personality is to psychology. Identity, remember, is the result of current and abandoned roles. Sexual identity is the result of the role of male or female as it is conceived and taught to human beings in particular societies, at particular times, and within particular segments of these societies.

Actually, however, sex roles, per se, do not exist. People do not relate to each other simply in their status of male or female. Sex-typed role expectations are always played out in combination with other roles (e.g., parent, spouse, lover, warrior, or teacher). Gender is most significant for the performance of family roles, but it permeates all other roles, particularly in societies characterized by extreme sex typing. A male teacher has the same formal rights and obligations as a female teacher in a particular educational setting., and yet in most societies he is not likely to perform his role as a woman would. He is likely to have different authority relationships with administrators, different relationships with students, and different conflicts about the role itself. He is seldom torn between his teaching obligations and homemaking and childrearing obligations, for example.

If females in a particular society are taught to be more emotionally expressive than males, typically, the women in that society are more likely to be expressive in their roles as parent, teacher, student, employee, friend, daughter, sister, wife, and lover. Gender is a basic status that has greater or less signifi-

cance for personality, motivation, and behavior in different social settings, depending very largely on learning, experience,
and the expectations of others.

When we talk about sex-typed differences, we are saying that
most men and women learn different roles, have different self
images or identities, and tend to think, act, and feel differently.
To know and explain how and why this happens is the goal of
much scientific research these days; to change the sex-typed
roles that people learn is an important goal of the contemporary
women's movement, around the world.

PURPOSE AND PLAN. Sociologists usually do not carry out
research and accumulate knowledge about human beings and
human societies simply because they are curious. Most sociologists hope that the information and understanding they provide
will be used—by government, particularly—to relieve human
conflict and suffering. Sociology does not thrive under oppres-
sive political regimes. Where there is an interest in reform, political leaders will want information about the needs and circumstances of the population, to give themselves a rational basis
for making changes. If we know that six million working women
in this country have children under six, and there are only
900,000 licensed, approved day care centers, a need is obvious
—to those who are concerned with human needs.

Of course sociological knowledge can also be used by those
who want to avoid reform or to enhance their power—thus
armed, they can manipulate, control, and propagandize more
effectively. For example, the knowledge of what people fear
most and which and how many people have a particular fear
can be used to win elections. This use has also been made of our
work. All sciences, including the science of society, can be used
to serve as well as to destroy humanitarian values.

With this caution in mind, we will look into the lives of men
and women in various parts of the world today. We will exam-

ine their problems and their anxieties—particularly as these stem from arbitrary, contradictory, confused, outmoded, or frustrating conceptions of their sexual identities.

We cannot say that a certain conception of masculinity or femininity is arbitrary unless we know what, if anything, is biologically inevitable about the emotions, thoughts, and behavior of men and women. Thus we begin with a discussion of the biological basis of sexual identity.

We cannot identify what is outmoded about current sex role conceptions without knowing how and why these conceptions have changed historically. Thus we look into conceptions of masculinity and femininity in hunting and gathering societies, in agricultural societies, and in industrialized societies. If we are able to locate the factors that have historically led to change in the way men and women have related to one another (e.g., developments in science and technology), we can better understand present contradictions and confusions in the relationships between the sexes.

Since we are concerned, ultimately, with influencing government policy and promoting rational planning to alleviate unnecessary conflict and suffering, we must understand the nature and the extent of problems that people have in relation to sexual identity. Such understanding, however, requires us to review differences in the way male and female infants are brought up in societies where we have this kind of information. We must try to judge the appropriateness of traditional sex roles and particular sex-typed personality traits for the demands and challenges of existence in modern societies. We must understand the changing conflicts of men and women as they mature and grow old. We must know why these conflicts arise and how extensive they are within the different classes, races, and generations. We must assess the status of women on a global basis. We must decide to what extent women are a minority group, if we use certain objective standards to make this judgment. We must understand the relationship between the self images that men and women are taught and the goals that they seek. If women believe themselves to be intellectually inferior to men, they are not likely to compete for the most demanding academic accomplishments. If men believe they are incapable of sentiment and warmth, they will not give or seek emotional support in family and friendship relationships.

To predict events and behavior, scientists develop generalizations and laws about the material and nonmaterial worlds. The chemist can predict that if two substances are placed together in a flask under certain controlled conditions, a third substance will be produced. Social scientists can predict also, although our predictions are much more precarious. If technological change, accumulated scientific knowledge, and government policy continue to proceed in certain directions, we can anticipate that childrearing practices, the degree of sex typing, and sexual identity will continue to be affected in certain ways.

Long-range predictions are unpopular now, as are planning and optimism, at least in the United States. My last chapter contains predictions about the future of sex typing and sex differences in human societies, nonetheless. Knowledge about human differences and why they exist promotes tolerance and change. We do what we can to ease the twin burdens of arbitrary cultural tradition and irrational circumstance which most people, male and female, have had to endure—in modern times and always.

2 | Biology and Sexual Identity

Men and women differ from each other anatomically, hormonally, and genetically. Anatomical differences involving average size, strength (ratio of muscle to fat), and reproductive organs, are obvious. These differences have almost always been a basis for assigning different chores and privileges to men and women. Men, who can usually run faster, throw farther, and hit harder, have been hunters and warriors; women, who give birth to children and nurse them, have usually also cared for them.

Hormone and chromosome differences between the sexes are less obvious. The question of the relationship of these differences to personality, sexual behavior, and conceptions of masculinity and femininity, is controversial and still open. I am including sexual behavior under the topic of the biological basis of sexual identity because the double standard, which permits nonmarital sexual freedom to men but not to women, is a norm that has often been justified on the grounds that men have a stronger sex drive than women. If men and women are taught and believe that they have different and unequal sex drives, this perspective becomes part of their self image, and it affects their sexual behavior significantly.

In trying to understand the relationship between biology and socially defined sexual identity, we start with what we know

about the obvious and not so obvious biological differences between the sexes. We must also review the data on experiments
with nonhumans, in which either biological factors (e.g., hormone levels) or environmental factors have been deliberately
modified. The effects on behavior of these changes then indicate
the relative weight of the two sets of factors in determining
behavior—among nonhumans, at least.

For humans, we look to natural or accidental variations in biology or environment. From studies of the behavior of men and
women who have abnormal chromosome structures or atypical
sex hormone balances, we derive some insight into the relationship between biological factors and the behavior we define as
masculine and feminine. But these individuals are atypical, after
all. Thus we look at differences in the personality traits and behavior of men and women under differing social conditions—in
different kinds of societies and in the same society at different
times. We then can approximate the actual and possible ranges
in the emotions, motivations, and behavior of men and women.
We also have good evidence about the possibility of overriding
biological predisposition, whatever this may be, if we find
strong differences in typical male or female behavior at different
times and in different societies. This kind of information is reviewed in detail in the next chapter, although we touch on it,
here and there, in this chapter.

It is very important to bear in mind that I am not trying to
answer the question of biology *versus* environment in establishing the sexual identities of men and women. This cannot be
done. The question, rather, involves the *relative* importance, or
weight, of each set of factors in determining typical male and female personality traits and role conceptions, as we now observe
them. Moreover, in reporting sex differences here and throughout the book, I am talking about statistically most frequent, or
typical, differences—in personality traits, for example. But "typical" simply means "possessed by or characterizing more than 50
per cent." The remaining men and women, who do not have a

particular personality trait, are therefore "atypical"; and this remaining number can be quite large.

What are these typical differences between the sexes, old and young, rich and poor, that have been observed, measured, praised, and bemoaned in contemporary societies? Generally, and despite many exceptions and much overlapping, more females than males are passive (less active, less overtly dominating and aggressive), dependent (helpless, conforming, obedient, suggestible), nurturing (helpful to others, sympathetic, and empathic), highly verbal, affiliative (sociable, popularity-oriented), and sexually restrained. More males are achievement-motivated (for power and fame in political and economic activities) and, in adulthood, are physically aggressive, emotionally inexpressive, and assertive about displaying and utilizing their intelligence (1).

Although sex role conceptions are changing, the foregoing differences between males and females in contemporary societies are still widespread, and they are still considered proper and desirable by most men and women (2). To what extent are these traits determined by chromosomes, hormones, and anatomy? Have they always been defined as masculine or feminine in all societies? How can we describe the behavior of men and women who have abnormally high levels of hormones that are usually more prevalent in the opposite sex (e.g., women who have very high androgen levels)? Do nonhuman males and females differ with respect to aggression or passivity, and if so, what relevance does this have to human sex differences?

MALE AND FEMALE BIOLOGICAL DIFFERENCES. A look at studies of human genetics is not very enlightening in answering the questions just posed because genes do not directly affect behavior. Chromosome differences may indirectly affect sex role behavior, however, since they affect the sex ratio. I will come back to this point in a moment.

Chromosome Differences. Females have two sex chromosomes (i.e., XX makeup); males have an X and a Y sex chromosome in every cell of their bodies. The composition of the Y chromosome is unknown, but the X chromosome seems to have an important protective effect on the susceptibility to infectious and noninfectious disease. Some investigators believe that the second X chromosome in females is an extra stand-in chromosome to replace defective chromosomes. However this genetic difference operates, fewer female fetuses are spontaneously aborted, the female infant mortality rate is lower, and women have a longer average life expectancy than men—this is true of females throughout the animal kingdom, incidentally. Females also have fewer genetically transmitted defects, such as hemophelia and color blindness, and they resist the effect of malnutrition and other kinds of physical deprivation better than males. (3). Biologically, it turns out, the weaker sex is not weaker, except in terms of muscular strength.

Of the various traits of temperament and ability that are defined as typically feminine or masculine, aggression and passivity are most apt to be regarded as possibly genetic in origin. A few investigators have recently found that a slightly higher proportion of males who are violently aggressive have an extra Y chromosome (chromosome pattern XYY) (4). Researchers have also reported greater passivity and low virility in males who have sex chromosomes X, X, and Y. These findings, however, require more confirmation. They do not deny the overwhelming evidence of the effects of learning and environment on the development of aggressive behavior in males; furthermore, the great majority of violently aggressive men have a normal genetic constitution.

One way—possibly the only way of interpreting such data—is to infer a biological predisposition, particularly when the same environment produces different effects on different individuals (e.g., two brothers, one of whom grows up to be a priest and the other a murderer). The difficulty with this kind of argument (which is quite common in the biological sciences) is that human environments—physical, social, and psychological—are extremely complex; and it is a scientific impossibility to judge that environmental influences are identical for any two individuals.

The predisposition argument, furthermore, avoids the basic question of the relative weights to be assigned to biology and to learning in determining motivation and behavior. How important is this predisposition? What does it take to overcome it? Suppose we can establish that experience and learning are more important than biological predisposition—and I think we can, for humans who are not atypical biologically. Is such a demonstration relevant?

Although the typical differences in male and female susceptibility to disease and death have little direct relevance to the personality traits defined as masculine or feminine in most societies, these differences do affect the sex ratio. A surplus of females exists in young adult and older age categories in the United States. The overall surplus of approximately six million women in American society, for example, can have indirect implications for sex-typed behavior. If men are in short supply, relatively, women are less apt to assert and assume traits that are presently considered unfeminine. This would apply particularly to such traits as aggression, independence, and achievement motivation, which at present are still strongly discouraged in females, especially in the white working class.

The future of the sex ratio, however, is likely to depend far more on scientific developments than on human genetics. The possibility of preselecting the sex of offspring will soon become a reality. This development will likely affect the sex ratio unfavorably, however. Birthrates and related trends are very difficult to predict. Social scientists did not anticipate the postwar baby boom in the United States, nor did they foresee the present all-time low in the birthrate. Most parents, according to the surveys, prefer at least two children: one male and one female. And if they could only have one child, they would prefer a male.

The imbalance in the sex ratio will probably increase when parents are actually able to choose the sex of their children. At the present time, more males than females are conceived and born. The natural sex ratio, which is diminished by the unequal survival rates of male and female infants, will be even higher when the sex of offspring can be determined in advance. With the drastically declining birthrate, only children will become more common; and unless present attitudes change, these only children will most likely be male if parents have a choice.

At the same time, progress will be made toward equalizing the life expectancies of men and women by continued developments in the cure and control of all types of diseases, particularly heart disease and cancer—the two major killers of middle and old age to which males are more susceptible. Biologists do not anticipate any great extension of the human life span unless the mystery of aging is discovered; but with anticipated advances, particularly in chemical therapy and organ replacement techniques, more males should be able to survive to the present outer limits of the life cycle.

Other factors are also involved here, however, especially the greater psychological stresses of economic achievement to which males, typically, have been more heavily exposed. Interestingly, a recent unpublished comparison of male and female death rates in the United States indicates a closing of the gap in urban areas, where women are more likely to be employed outside the home. The larger the city, the greater the percentage of women employed in jobs usually sex-typed for males; and the higher the percentage of employed women, the lower the gap between male and female death rates (5). In societies where women do not outlive men (e.g., in India, Guatemala, and Ceylon), we can infer that the practice of female infanticide or neglect of female infants continues, informally and illegally.

Hormone Differences. Much more information—and much more controversy—exists on male and female hormone differences and their possible relationship to sex-typed roles and identities than on chromosome differences. That hormones affect such factors as sexual drive and temperament has been rather well established for primates and lower animal forms—and for humans, in the case of hormone abnormality, somewhat less certainly. The source of controversy, again, lies in the relative weight that should be given to hormonal factors, as opposed to environment and learning, in accounting for the typical role behavior of the majority of men and women. Those who believe that humans are not bound by their hormones note that the cortex, which is the seat of memory and learning in animals, comprises 90 per cent of the human brain. They argue, therefore, that biological predisposition is relatively unimportant in humans, since they have so much greater capacity to learn and to be influenced by their environment.

And yet serious investigators continue to reach completely opposite conclusions about this question: "The cortex has not emancipated man from hormonal influence" (6), or "We suggest that the evolutionary decrease in the importance of gonadal hormones reflects a compensatory increase in the degree of control over such activities by the cortex of the brain . . . (7) Particularly in the case of man, the role of learning is paramount" (8). Which is true?

Hormones are chemical substances that are produced in the endocrine glands—the pituitary gland, the thyroid gland, the pancreatic inlets, and the gonads (ovaries and testes). The pituitary gland controls endocrine levels but is itself under the control of the hypothalamus, thus is influenced by the higher centers of the brain—a very important recent discovery which supports the idea that the cortex can override hormonal predispositions in human beings.

Hormones regulate various bodily processes—metabolism and growth rates, for example, and the development of the primary sex characteristics. At puberty the sex hormones trigger the enlargement of the penis and scrotum and the development of ejaculatory capacity in males, and the onset of menstruation and the development of analogous genital structures, the clitoris and labia majora, in females. The development of secondary sex characteristics is also controlled by hormone action—the enlargement of the breasts and pelvis and the growth of pubic and axillary hair in females, and voice and skeletal changes and the appearance of pubic, axillary, and facial hair in males.

In the male the most important hormone for developing and maintaining biological sex characteristics is testosterone, one of a group known as the androgens. In adulthood, normal males produce about six times as much testosterone as females. In the female, the estrogens and progesterone are most significant for the development and regulation of biological sex characteristics.

Actually, to label the androgens and estrogens "male" or "female" sex hormones is misleading, since both types of hormones are produced by men and women, but in differing amounts. These differences, furthermore, do not become significant until puberty, when hormone production accelerates dramatically as a result of the development of the central nervous system. Infants and children of both sexes produce only a small quantity of sex hormones.

In utero, however, the production by the fetus of androgenic hormones (at approximately the sixth week of embryonic development) determines male differentiation. The fetus is initially female in potential. Without the intervention of androgenic hormones the fetus develops into a female—which is the basic form of the mammalian embryo (9). This is significant as a boost to female pride, and also because biologically oriented investigators have concluded that the interplay of sex hormones in the fetus not only determines gender identity, but influences postnatal behavior in the direction we label masculine or feminine (10).

An example of the type of research that has been done on

nonhumans to illuminate this problem is the injection of testosterone into pregnant female monkeys resulting in female offspring that display much of the behavior commonly seen in young male monkeys: a higher level of energy and activity, as revealed in more rough and tumble pursuit and sex play, more threat behavior, and fewer withdrawal responses in the face of threat. This type of behavior persists for up to three years in the offspring of injected monkeys, indicating a durable postnatal effect on the female progeny. In other studies, the injection of testosterone in adult male monkeys has been found to alter previously established dominance patterns among male monkeys. Notable exceptions notwithstanding, moreover, field studies indicate that females throughout the animal kingdom are more apt to engage in passifying, grooming behavior and are generally more nurturing toward the young of the species (11).

Most researchers do not believe that prenatal hormone action is more influential than learning experiences in determining the later behavior of human beings; some argue, however, that the prenatal effects of the sex hormones on the hypothalamus establish differential susceptibility to environmental stimuli in later life. Based on research on nonhumans, they feel that males have a greater tendency to react with aggressive responses and females with passive responses because of these differences in prenatal hormone activity. It is claimed that it is as legitimate to draw analogies between human and nonhumans on the effects of prenatal hormones on behavior as it is to apply the results of drug research on lower animals to humans. This argument is questionable, however, since learning experiences, which are irrelevant in the physiological response to drugs, are not irrelevant to the development of personality in human beings.

One final argument casts doubt on the claim that prenatal sex hormones significantly affect sex-typed behavior in humans. Studies of newborn infants do not show consistent and measurably large, average differences in sensitivity to various stimuli, activity patterns, and frustration tolerance between male and female infants. Much more research needs to be done in this area, but since results are not convincingly consistent and since quite opposite findings are reported by different researchers, it appears either that some investigators are biased or that there are, in fact, no such *typical* differences in the behavior of newborn males and females.

In adult males and females, testosterone levels appear to influence the strength of the sex drive. In women, most of the male hormones are secreted by the adrenal glands. Women who have had their adrenal glands removed, report a dramatic loss in sexual responsiveness. The removal of the ovaries, which diminishes estrogen levels, has no reported effect on sexual drive.

A marked increase in sexual responsiveness has been reported by women who have been given massive doses of testosterone in the treatment of breast cancer. On the other hand, males do not consistently respond to testosterone injections with increased sexual drive. Impotence is largely, if not entirely, psychological in origin. The problem is complicated further by the observed rise in testosterone levels in humans and in nonhumans when they experience an increase in sexual or aggressive activity. Which is the cart and which is the horse?

The results of most studies of the effects of hormone treatment on behavior and motivation must be viewed with caution, since the element of suggestibility complicates the findings. People usually know what kind of treatment they are getting. We need additional, carefully controlled studies in which placebos as well as hormones are used alternatively in otherwise comparable groups. Then, too, studies done on individuals with pathological hormone levels may have little applicability to individuals who fall within the normal hormone range. The biological predisposition would be far less strong for these individuals, and psychological factors that much more important.

Additional insight into the general question of the importance of biology in sex-typed behavior comes from research on transsexuals—individuals who identify with and adopt the sex-typed personality traits of the opposite sex. For psychological reasons, or because the structure of the genitalia is ambiguous at birth, due to prenatal hormone abnormality, transsexuals are brought up by their parents as members of the sex to which they do not belong, biologically.

John Money and his associates at Johns Hopkins Medical School, who have spent years researching and treating this problem, have concluded that sexual identity and sex-typed behavior is established primarily by learning experiences in the first three years of life (the "critical period"). They feel that after 18 months, it would be ill-advised to attempt to change the assigned sex of a child whose gender identity was mistaken at birth (12).

Male Aggression. Aggression is a trait that has been defined as masculine in almost all societies. Historically, in a majority of societies, males have been required to suppress emotions related to love, and females have been required to suppress emotions related to hate. To what extent, then, is male aggression innate and genetically programmed (13)? This is an important question, bearing on the supposed inevitability of war and the ultimate fate of the human animal.

In nonhumans, testosterone levels are quite clearly related to aggressive behavior. Male monkeys which are at the top of the dominance hierarchies in their colonies tend to have the highest levels of testosterone. The injection of testosterone in nonhumans increases aggressive behavior. To jump from this kind of evidence to an assumption of an innate "killer" instinct in males, however, is not valid. The heightened aggression that correlates with high testosterone levels in nonhumans is a reaction to a stronger sex drive. It does not establish the existence of an independent, nonreactive, spontaneous aggressive instinct in man.

Biological explanations for human shortcomings and suffering have always been popular with the privileged and the conservative, who have used these arguments to block humanistic reforms and planned social change. If biology will out, and the sexes, the races, and the classes are not born equal, intellectually or temperamentally, there is no point in equalitarian political and economic policies.

Individuals are not born equal, biologically. They differ in intelligence and temperament. But biological justifications for giving superior privileges to large categories of human beings, because they happen to have been born female, black, or poor, cannot be proved. If opportunity were absolutely equal for all individuals, regardless of family origin, race, or gender, we could argue that those at the top belong there because they are innately brighter or more aggressive. We could then argue that women, as a group, are not and have not been leaders in human societies because they are biologically less aggressive.

Since perfect equality of opportunity for both sexes has not existed, at least in agricultural and industrial societies, we have to look to reasons other than innate differences in aggressive instincts between men and women to explain the historically superior power of men. But first we must review the evidence against the existence of an innate killer instinct in males (14). If this instinct does not exist, we have eliminated one of the arguments for the inevitability of patriarchy in human societies.

Physiologists have not been able to demonstrate the existence of chemical or other physical changes in animals, comparable to the drop in blood sugar levels as hunger mounts, that would indicate a buildup of aggressive energy, independent of the external environment. Animals act aggressively in response to external stimuli. Furthermore, an innate impulse to kill, simply for the sake of killing, would hinder survival in the evolutionary process. Natural selection would be unlikely to operate in the direction of establishing traits that would put animals into unnecessary danger. Animals kill to satisfy hunger needs and to defend themselves; they do not kill because of jealousy, rivalry, or pleasure. Humans elaborate the notion of killing for survival, often irrationally, but this is not proof of innate predisposition.

Territorial defense patterns, which are a means of establishing differential food and sexual privileges in animal (nonhuman) groups, involve threatening gestures rather than killing. *Homo sapiens*' closest collateral relatives, the nonhuman primates, furthermore, are not usually belligerent unless provoked. According to the archaeological evidence, even the hominids—animal forms from which *Homo sapiens* directly evolved—did not kill to satisfy a "predatory instinct." They killed to satisfy their hunger needs.

Psychologists have accumulated a vast body of data indicating that much of the aggression expressed by human beings is a reactive response to frustration—the blocking of needs or goal-directed behavior. If aggression is universal in human societies, it is because frustration is universal. Social conditions affect the level of frustration in the population. The culture defines the objects of aggression and encourages or inhibits the expression of aggression—differently for males and females, usually.

Males have almost always been allowed to express aggression more freely than females because the ultimate expression of aggression is physical force. Males, who are typically larger and stronger, can express overt aggression more effectively than females. Caspar Milquetoast is always portrayed as shorter and physically weaker than his wife. In this sense, sex-typed role conceptions would be an adaptation to ultimate male and female biological differences. And these differences are hormonal in origin, since androgen levels affect size and strength.

The above-mentioned male–female biological difference probably underlies the fact that no true matriarchy has ever been known to exist in human societies. Even in matrilineal societies, where descent, property, and group membership is transmitted through the female line, and women have a somewhat higher status relative to men, actual authority is vested in male members of the matrilineal clans—the wife's maternal uncle, brother, or grown son, typically.

Anthropologists have reported on societies in which both

males and females appear to be equally aggressive, on societies in which both sexes are equally passive, and on societies in which females are more overtly aggressive than males. A classic study in this area is Margaret Mead's, *Sex and Temperament in Three Primitive Societies*, (15), but other investigators have also reported on a few small, nonliterate societies in which aggression was prohibited or prescribed by the culture for both sexes equally, or where our sex-typed cultural norms were reversed.

Dr. Mead, in her study of three small New Guinea villages located within 200 miles of one another, does not claim that there are no innate male and female differences in temperament—the basic emotions of love and hate and the personality traits that derive from them. Her purpose, rather, is to illustrate the plasticity of human biology. Among the Arapash, for example, the anthropologist found that both sexes were gentle and maternal, oriented toward the growth of all living things—children, animals, fetuses (the Arapash believed that human semen feeds the fetus)—and toward the needs of those other than the self. Aggressiveness, competitiveness, and possessiveness were strongly discouraged for both sexes, and gentleness, passivity, emotional warmth, and volatility were non-sex-typed, ideal personality traits. Sex typing was also minimal in the area of child care, which was defined as the work of both men and women (16). Both sexes were regarded as having identical sex drives; they were equally free and equally likely to initiate sexual intercourse (17).

In contrast, among the cannibal and headhunting Mundugumor, both males and females were violently aggressive, insatiably acquisitive, and equally rivalrous. On the question of the survival of a hormonally based maternal instinct in the human female, Mundugumor women, at least, revealed no such instinct. They dreaded pregnancy, nursed unwillingly, and violently rejected their daughters—who might someday be used by the husband in trade for a second wife. Dr. Mead feels that only the great wealth and natural resources of this society enabled it to exist at all, characterized as it was by universal hostility and distrust. Both sexes hated openly and loved aggressively.

For the Arapash and the Mundugumor, sex typing was minimal; men and women had very similar temperaments. Among the Tchambuli, sex typing and sex differences were strong. Many of the traits we define as feminine, however, were regarded as masculine in this society. Men were artistic, gossipy, delicate, and emotional; women were the major economic providers and were energetic, managerial, and unadorned.

Dr. Mead's methods and conclusions have been questioned by some investigators. Other evidence, however, particularly from agricultural societies, indicates that love and hate and their derivatives in personality traits (nurturance or aggression) are primarily a result of learning and environment. Men have loved and have been tender and sentimental, openly and without shame; and women have been aggressive, equally with men, when permitted and encouraged to do so in the process of growing up in their particular societies.

Hormone Cycles. All animals, human and nonhuman, male and female, are subject to cyclical changes in hormone levels. These cycles occur daily, near-monthly, seasonally, and annually (18). A number of studies in America and elsewhere have established an association between estrogen levels and mood changes as reported by female subjects. Similar findings have been claimed in a few studies of primates, although results have by no means been conclusive. Generally, these studies have indicated that high levels of estrogen are correlated with positive emotions in women, and low levels (during the premenstrual phase of the menstrual cycle) are associated with negative emotions such as hostility, depression, and anxiety about death, mutilation, or abandonment (19).

In contrast, and curiously, only a few studies have attempted to relate cyclical mood states in males to changing androgen levels. The studies that do exist have also indicated fluctuations in anxiety, aggressiveness, irritability, and depression in men, corresponding to changes in androgen levels over periods of approximately one month (20). Why have there been so few studies on male hormone cycles? Very likely, at least part of the answer is that males, typically, are likely to hide mood swings and feelings of vulnerability far more successfully than females. Traditional conceptions of masculinity require the male to be stoical and brave.

It has long been believed that females are more fearful and more neurotic than males in our society. More women than men seek medical and psychological help for the same physical and mental problems. But are women, typically, more psychologically vulnerable than men? On this question, more recent and careful research suggests that the presumed sex differences in emotional stability are at least partly mythical. Females are permitted greater freedom to admit and express suffering or weakness. Defensiveness is a crucial and often overlooked factor in studies of sex differences in emotional states. Objective measures of anxiety, such as tests of galvanic skin response (a physiological measure of anxiety), do not reveal significant differences in male and female anxiety levels under experimental fear-inducing situations, although most females score higher in verbal expressions of fear in these situations. (21).

Projective tests such as the Rorschach (ink blot) test and the Thematic Apperception Test (tell a story about the picture), which attempt to get around the problem of male defensiveness by tapping unconscious fantasies and impulses, indicate generally that more American males than females are anxious (22). This would certainly seem to be a reasonable finding, given the more challenging existence that males typically experience in our society. Cross-cultural Rorschach data, incidentally, also reveal higher levels of anxiety in most males (23).

As for the question of the relative emotional stability of the sexes, we can cite the results of a large-scale, door-to-door study conducted in midtown Manhattan in 1962. In this attempt to assess the actual incidence of psychological problems in a large urban (white) population, no significant overall differences in psychological adjustment were found between the sexes. Typical symptoms varied, however, for each sex (24).

Changes in mood state corresponding to hormone changes in both men and women are strongly affected by psychological factors. Except at the extreme of hormone abnormality, moreover, these mood changes are not so severe that they have any necessary implication for behavior. Depression, irritability, and anxiety arising from conditions having nothing to do with biological rhythms can be far more crippling to human functioning. Finally, these effects do not seem to occur in societies where there is no knowledge of the possible effects of hormone changes on mood.

Women in nonliterate societies apparently did not experience premenstrual tension or postmenopausal depression (when estrogen levels decline), although in industrial societies both phenomena have been found in a variety of cultures (25). Postmenopausal depression is very closely related to role loss in industrial societies—the loss of the mother role, particularly, after the youngest child has left home. In traditional societies (nonliterate and agricultural) this role was not lost because adult children were not likely to move away from the village or family compound. The care of grandchildren in the days of the extended family was an important obligation of the middle-aged woman, an obligation that occupied her for the remainder of her relatively short life span. In modern, industrialized society, women who are gainfully employed or who are otherwise very active and committed to nonfamily enterprises, are less apt to experience postmenopausal depression than women who live more traditional lives.

Anatomical Differences. The anatomical differences between men and women, especially as these affect strength and reproductive functioning, have been much more frequently and ob-

viously linked to sex role conceptions than have chromosome or
hormone differences. Even here, however, some cultures have
ignored the obvious, defining women as having stronger heads
or backs, for example, and therefore assigning to women the task
of carrying heavy burdens.

Anatomy and Sexual Behavior. As societies develop technologically, and as animal, wind, water, electric, and machine power
increasingly supplant human muscle and brain power, the average differences in the size and strength of the sexes diminish in
importance for determining the sexual division of labor. The
same is true for the differences in reproductive organs and functioning. The assignment of infant care to mothers becomes less a
matter of biological necessity and more a matter of choice, for
the masses as well as for the elite. In economically stratified societies, aristocratic and upper class women have always dele-
gated the care of their children to others. In highly industrialized societies, this choice in sex role behavior is extended to
other classes (voluntarily in most nations), as infant care comes
to be regarded increasingly as an extension of the educational
function of government.

Nevertheless, and incidentally, this does not represent a decline in sex typing, because child care continues to be defined as
primarily a feminine task. Increasingly, however, it need not be
a full-time imperative for the woman who assumes the role of
mother.

Anatomy has also been regarded as having great significance
for the sex drive and for the typical differences in personality of
the sexes in our society. Throughout history, appropriately
enough, human conceptions about the respective sex drives of
women and men have varied in relation to the relative freedom
of the two sexes to initiate sexual contact and to engage in nonmarital intercourse. The significant factor here has been economics, however, not anatomy. In hunting and gathering nonliterate societies, where all were poor or where families were not
greatly differentiated with respect to wealth (the level of tech-

nological development did not permit the accumulation of a large economic surplus), men and women were usually equally active sexually (26).

In agricultural societies, economic differences among families become extreme, and biological paternity and inheritance along biological family lines become very significant. The mating of offspring is controlled (by arranged marriage) to increase family power and wealth. The sexual activity of women is more rigorously suppressed (confined, ideally, to procreation), and women come to be regarded, conveniently, as having a weaker sex drive.

The Arab countries were unusual in that they believed that women were potentially more erotic than men. In these societies, the practice of clitoridectomy (the surgical removal of the clitoris) represented an attempt to curb this stronger drive, and indicated an awareness of the importance, recently rediscovered in this country, of the clitoris in the sexual response of the human female.

Women of the lower classes in economically stratified traditional societies were less rigidly controlled by their families in their premarital sexual activities. Chaperoning was more difficult, particularly if poorer women worked outside the home as domestics. Whether they enjoyed sex more is unknown. We have no Kinsey studies on traditional societies. Very few women were literate. The women (in the upper class) who were literate rarely wrote about their sexual escapades, and those who did usually did not dwell on their sexual enjoyment.

In the nineteenth century it was commonly believed that women of the lower classes experienced greater sexual gratification. The rich and the powerful attributed the freer sexual behavior and the presumed greater enjoyment of sex by lower class women to their closer biological relationship to nonhuman animals. The poor, as well as women of the nonwhite races, were believed to represent a lower stage in the evolutionary process.

Recent studies of the sexual responsiveness of women in var-

ious classes in contemporary societies indicate that poverty does
not promote sexual gratification in economically stratified societies. The higher the class, in fact, the more likely women are to
enjoy sex. And since the mid-1960s, at least, middle and upper
class young women have been experiencing a relatively sharp
increase in premarital sexual freedom.

For a number of reasons, sexual freedom for women increases
in highly industrial societies. Familism declines as women and
children are able to earn independent income in the nonfamily
corporate economy. Many of the family's traditional functions in
the area of education, welfare, health, and protection are shared
or taken over by the government. Parents lose their monopolis-
tic control over their children's behavior—including their sexual
behavior. The marital choices of offspring become less vital to
the perpetuation of the family line. The status of women rises
(as they become more independent economically and as they
achieve higher levels of education); control over unwanted
births increases, and the double standard declines. Restrictions
on the nonmarital sexual behavior of women diminish, and so
do notions of a weaker sex drive in women.

Recently, in fact, it has been claimed on anatomical grounds
that women have a stronger sex drive than males—an insatiable, multiorgasmic drive comparable to that of other female primates when they are in heat. Mary Jane Sherfey, basing her
conclusions on the finding by William Masters and Virginia
Johnson that women subjects report multiple orgasms as a result
of clitoral masturbation, has claimed that the female sexual
drive is insatiable. She suggests that the institution of the family
evolved to control this drive and that if the current decline in
the sexual restraint of women continues, ". . . a return to the
rigid enforced repression will be inevitable and mandatory. Otherwise the biological family will disappear and what other patterns of infant care and adult relationships could adequately
substitute, can not now be imagined" (27).

Dr. Sherfey also concludes, on the basis of Masters and Johnson's finding that the clitoris and the lower third of the vagina operate inseparably as a source of genital orgasmic response in the female, that the clitorial tip (glans) is, in fact, a stronger and more sensitive erogenous zone than the lower third of the vagina (28).

As a reaction to the severe sexual repression historically experienced by females, particularly in the West, Dr. Sherfey's claims are understandable. As scientific data, however, they are contradicted by other data. Nonhuman female primates have little reason to divert their energies into nonsexual outlets while they are in heat. It is difficult to imagine the human female, with her far more complex learning experiences and her elaborate system of symbolic meanings, cathexes, and sublimated activities, pursuing sexual "satiation in insatiation." This is described as follows for nonhuman female primates by Dr. Sherfey:

> Having no cultural restrictions, these primate females will perform coitus from 20 to 50 times a day during the peak week of estrus (heat), usually with several series of copulation in rapid succession. If necessary, they will flirt, solicit, present and stimulate the male in order to obtain successive coitions. They will "consort" with one male for several days until he is exhausted then take up with another. They will emerge from periods of heat totally exhausted, often with wounds from spent males who have repulsed them. I suggest that something akin to this behavior could be paralleled by the human female if her civilization allowed it (29).

My suggestion is that the highly evolved human cortex and the elaborated needs and goals of human beings, some of them deriving indirectly from the sex drive, would not allow such behavior, whatever the cultural definition of female sexuality in human societies. Anthropological evidence indicates that even in societies characterized by the most sexual freedom and the largest amount of leisure, sexual intercourse occurred, usually,

once daily, for both sexes (30). Women in these societies did not
begin to approach the behavior of nonhuman female primates
in heat.

It is difficult to imagine, furthermore, that the evolutionary
process would result in the establishment of the clitoris as the
primary erogenous zone in human females, as Dr. Sherfey
claims. This would discourage heterosexual genital contact, endanger reproduction, and imperil the survival of the species.
Masters and Johnson did not find the clitoris to be more sensitive than the vagina; both organs are inseparably involved in
the sexual act. Moreover, what were reported as multiple orgasms by Masters and Johnson's subjects occurred *only* as a result of clitoral masturbation. These so-called multiple orgasms
were subjectively experienced as a succession of "tingly" sensa-
tions of a less intense nature than a maximal orgasm. The latter
type of explosive orgasm, which is identical in pelvic muscular
response with male orgasm, occurred only *once* in female subjects (31). They then experienced a satiation and required a re-
covery period similar to that of the male. This finding has been
ignored by Dr. Sherfey and by many writers who have followed
her lead in discussions of multiple orgasms in women.

Information from nonliterate societies does not support the
claim of female insatiability. In societies lacking the double
standard and having few restrictions on sexual activity, females
have been as active as males and as likely to initiate sexual contact, but they have not been *more* active sexually (32).

The question of the relative strength of the biological sex
drive in males and females cannot be answered at the moment.
The androgens seem to be very important to the strength of the
sex drive, and androgen levels are higher in males. Here too,
there is controversy, however. Replacement therapy in cases of
androgen deficiency does not heighten the sex drive consistently
in all subjects. Psychological factors and suggestibility seem to
play a very significant role in the results of replacement therapy.

It is fair to conclude, I feel, particularly on the basis of the anthropological evidence, that learning and cultural factors are paramount in the determination of sexual behavior for the great majority of humans, regardless of biological predisposition and whatever such predisposition may be typically for males and females.

Other aspects of the work of Masters and Johnson, incidentally, will have tremendous consequences for sex role conceptions and sexual behavior once certain findings become generally known. Masters and Johnson have found that the clitoris is very important in female orgasmic response. They have found that the size of the penis, when erect, does not vary much in males. They have concluded that the length of the penis is irrelevant, in any case, since only the lower third of the vagina is highly sensitive to sexual stimulation.

Such discoveries will relieve anxieties and promote more gratifying sexual techniques in our society.

Males will stop being anxious about their relative anatomical adequacy, and the female-on-top sexual position is likely to become more popular, since clitoral stimulation is more direct with this position. Nonliterate peoples knew this; they did not define the female-superior position as unfeminine until Christian missionaries came along, enlightened them, and introduced the male-superior or "missionary" position.

As the human brain evolved, women gained vastly greater independence from their hormones and, therefore, acquired a continuous sex drive. Women no longer had to be in heat to be sexually responsive. The greater development of the cortex also gave humans the capacity for language and the need for lengthy care and teaching by stable adult figures. Thus as the brain evolved, the family arose to control the continuous sex drive of both men and women and to provide stable caretakers for the human young. The incest taboo developed to curb the jealousy, conflict, and rivalry that would be caused by unrestricted sexual access between mother and son, father and daughter, or brother and sister, since such conflicts would endanger the biologically grounded need for prolonged care and instruction of the human young.

Monogamy became practical when sexual contact was no longer limited entirely, or almost entirely (as with nonhuman female primates) to the period when the female is in heat. The human male did not need to shop around, at least for biological reasons, with the desperate urgency of his nonhuman ancestors. If the elephant were monogamous, his mate would be available to him once a year. Humans are beyond all that; they can tolerate monogamy, at least ideally.

Anatomy and Personality.   The differences in male and female bodily structures have also been regarded as having necessary implications for personality and sexual identity. This position has been particularly favored by classical psychoanalysts. Erik Erikson, for example, has claimed that the female's productive "inner-bodily space" (the womb), her anatomical breast-feeding structures, the receptive vagina, and the stationary ovum which passively receives the active, intrusive penis and the mobile sperm cell, directly result in a greater tendency for the female to be generous and tranquil. Her anatomy predestines her to a life centering on family obligations and the "indoors of houses" (the indoors of houses being analogous to the womb). On the other hand, the personality and sex role imperatives of male anatomy are active mastery and high achievement motivation in "the great outdoors of adventure" (33).

This type of formulation, unfortunately, ignores culture and learning as these affect our reactions to our bodies. For example, the biological fact of puberty, which begins with menstruation in the female, typically produces reactions of anxiety in our culture. The female is viewed as wounded, cursed, unclean, or sick. In other societies, and sometimes in our own society, the onset of menstruation is viewed with great elation and excitement, as a symbol of the attainment of a highly valued adulthood.

Receptivity in the sexual act, moreover, is not the equivalent of passivity. Women have been quite active, sexually and otherwise, in many societies, including our own. Active, aggressive women, in fact, are more responsive sexual partners.

Erikson's theory is partly derived from Freud's theories of psychosexual development—namely, that female anatomy (the reproductive structures generally and the lack of a penis in particular) results in female envy (of the penis), passivity, masochism, and a weaker superego. Inevitably, and as a consequence of these reproductive structures, it was believed that women were characterized by other related traits, such as a lesser capacity for impartial judgment, weaker social interests, and a lower ability to sublimate sexual drive in the form of creative and achievement activities (34). For example, Freud attributed weaker superego development in the female to a lack of a fear of castration (since females were already castrated). This fear in males, he believed, results in the resolution of the Oedipus complex and an internalization of the adult moral standards that make up the superego.

Freud's theories about the biological basis of certain personality traits in women are not supported by data from anthropology, history, sociology, and psychology. Recent studies of sex differences in superego development, for example, indicate that more females than males have strong superegos. This finding is attributed to the generally warmer and less authoritarian relationship that exists between parents and their female children (35).

The other personality traits (passivity, masochism, dependence) insofar as they appear to be more typical of females than males, can be shown to be related to different learning experiences—experiences that begin at the moment of birth and continue quite consistently for most women and men, throughout their lifetimes.

Freud also believed that the clitoris is superseded by the vagina as the "primary erogenous zone" in the adult female (36).

This assumption has also been shown to be incorrect, most recently in the research of Masters and Johnson, as I mentioned earlier. The two structures are inseparably involved in the orgasmic response of the human female.

Freud and the Freudians, orthodox and neo-Freudian, have come under considerable attack in recent years for their theories of femininity and for the effects these theories are believed to have had on female sexual identity and behavior in this country. Since psychoanalytic theory has probably been more influential in America than anywhere else in the world, and since it is a biologically grounded theory, it is important to try to evaluate the theory and its effects on the changing status, self images, and sexual behavior of women in the United States over the past fifty years.

It seems far more probable that the changes that have occurred in the status of women in America, as well as the injustices that remain, are due to developments in technology and science and to the economic and political conditions that have accompanied these developments, rather than to the influence of psychoanalytic theory. In fact, modifications in the theory and swings in its popularity can best be understood as a product of the changing economic and political context in America. It is customary in sociology to locate ideas as well as people in time and place. We explain why certain ideas or theories arise and become popular during certain periods of history. And we can do this for psychoanalytic theory. But first let us examine the theory itself.

Freud's conceptions of feminine personality were never as rigid as they have been portrayed to be. He cautioned that although "women may prefer passive behavior on the basis of sexual function . . . we must beware in this of understanding the influence of social customs, which similarly force women into passive situations" (37). In his paper on "Femininity," he stressed the bisexuality of human beings: "an individual is not a man or a woman, but always both . . . merely a certain amount of one

more than another" (38). In his essay "Some Psychical Consequences of the Anatomical Distinction Between the Sexes," he
emphasized, once again, the "bisexual disposition" of the human
animal "so that pure masculinity and femininity remain theoretical constructions of uncertain content" (39).

The concept of penis envy is no longer in use by most prac-
ticing psychoanalysts. It matters little, furthermore, if penis envy
is taken as literally true or if it is interpreted as symbolically
representing female envy of the superior power, privilege, and
prestige of males, as Karen Horney, Clara Thompson, and other
neo-Freudians long ago suggested. The concept of penis envy
is obnoxious to modern ears, but the concept of womb envy,
also formulated by psychoanalysts, is virtually unknown. Why
has this aspect of neo-Freudian theory not been publicized?
Dr. Bruno Bettelheim is criticized for his statement: ". . . we
must start with the realization that, as much as women want
to be good scientists and engineers, they want first and foremost
to be womanly companions to men and to be mothers" (40). In
Symbolic Wounds, however, his focus is on male envy of
women, particularly in horticultural, nonliterate societies (where
women tend to have relatively higher status), as this envy is
revealed in such practices as the couvade and male subincision (41).

In one society that practiced the custom of the couvade, pregnant women worked up until a few hours before birth. They
then retreated to a secluded spot, gave birth with the aid of a
few women attendants, and returned to work again in a short
time. As soon as the child was born, the father took to bed with
the baby, was nursed and given special food, and was excused
from the obligation to work for days and sometimes weeks. Dr.
Bettelheim concludes: "Women, emotionally satisfied by giving
birth and secure in their ability to produce life can agree to the
couvade; men need it to fill the emotional vacuum created by
their inability to bear children" (42).

The practice of subincision involved the slitting of the male urethra along the underside of the penis, creating a vulva-like opening. Once the operation was performed (and it was a voluntary procedure in the tribes in which it was found), the male was required to urinate in a squatting position as women do. The wound, incidentally, was often reopened and caused to bleed, in apparent imitation of the periodic menstruation of women. Dr. Bettelheim commented: "What needs to be satisfied is the desire of both men and women to play a significant part in the duties, obligations and prerogatives, the activities and enjoyments, that in our society happen to be thought of as belonging to the opposite sex" (43). Envy between the sexes is a two-way street that varies according to the relative status of the sexes in different societies at different times.

The emphasis in psychoanalytic theory on the importance of early childhood in psychological development, on the harmful consequences of maternal deprivation in infancy and childhood, and on the innate and biologically grounded passivity and dependence of women, served the ideological needs of American society during the economic depression of the 1930s and in the postwar period of the 1940s. It was essential for economic reasons to discourage the gainful employment of women during these periods, particularly at higher occupational levels. But times and economic conditions and needs have changed. Women are now needed in the labor force, especially in the white collar sector—in secretarial work, bookkeeping, selling—where personnel shortages persist.

The emphasis now in the social sciences is on a stable, loving substitute (if the mother is not available), the quality rather than the quantity of mother–child contact, and the importance of the father as well as the mother in psychological development.

As times have changed, so have ideologies and economic needs. Science generally and psychoanalysis in particular have been used and have been affected by changing social circumstances. These changing circumstances determine the knowledge that is sought at any given time and, very often, the conclusions that are reached. Facts are facts, but interpretations of facts are often culture bound.

The joys of sexuality, maternity, and mature love were never proscribed by psychoanalytic theory. The fulfillment of the creative and achievement needs of females are not currently proscribed by any but the most conservative of classical psychoanalysts. The ultimate standard for psychoanalytic treatment has always been self fulfillment. Cultural definitions of the nature and content of fulfillment change, as societies and cultures change. More recently, psychoanalytic practice has reflected these changes. It is now recognized that whatever the biological differences between males and females, there is no necessary relationship between these differences and sex role conceptions— certainly not in a push-button technology where even the basic differences in size and strength between males and females become increasingly irrelevant.

Other controversial aspects of psychoanalytic theory—the Freudian distinction between the clitoris and the vagina as the primary erogenous zone in female orgasm, for example—are but a storm in a tea cup. This relatively minor aspect of Freud's theoretical contributions was tentatively formulated. In his essay on female sexuality, moreover, he stated that "the clitoris, with its virile character, continues to function in later female sex life in a manner which is variable and is certainly not yet satisfactorily understood" (44). In any event, for the masses of American women this specific theory about the relative importance of various organs in feminine orgasm never had the widespread ideological consequences that is often attributed to it. Most women were not even aware of this particular aspect of Freud's theory of feminine sexuality.

What did make its way into the popular culture is the wider body of Freudian theory—the emphasis on the strength and importance of the human sex drive (in females as well as in males), on the pathological consequences of sexual repression, and on the importance of infantile sexuality as a natural precursor to healthy adult heterosexual behavior. These ideas have had enormous consequences for both female and male sexual behavior and identity in this country.

Expectations with respect to sexual behavior are an important aspect of cultural definitions of sex roles. The double standard arises historically as societies become economically stratified, as I pointed out earlier. Lower class women have always been allowed more premarital sexual freedom than have females of upper strata families, since virginity was essential to family-arranged matches that would enhance the family's power and wealth, and since fidelity assured inheritance within the biological family line.

In modern times, and largely for economic reasons, patriarchy and familism decline. Technology develops, allowing family members to be independently employed and women to achieve independent means, as their services in the nonfamily corporate economy become increasingly essential. The double standard declines with the decline of familism, and sex role conceptions begin to reflect this decline.

The shift from a production-oriented society to a consumption-oriented society, in countries characterized by high levels of technological development, is accompanied by an emphasis on impulse gratification, including sexual gratification for both sexes. Increasingly, the fun ethic competes with the work ethic. The sexual liberation of women is a very important aspect of psychological liberation, and psychoanalytic theory in this area has been a most significant factor in the liberation of women, not to mention men. In fact, it provided one source for the ideology for the sexual revolution in the United States.

The sexual revolution, which actually began in the 1920s, was primarily a result of developments in science and technology that gave increased control over contraception and venereal disease and provided the automobile and commercial forms of recreation. Such new institutions as movie theatres promoted the practice of dating and, at the same time, broke down the system of family chaperonage. Psychoanalytic theory, with its emphasis on the harmful affects of sexual repression and the discrepancies between attitudes toward childhood sexuality and requirements of adult sexuality in our society, was extremely influential in this revolution.

The trend toward the sexual liberation of women is far from complete. The very existence of a controversy over the nature, source, and frequency of orgasm in women is at least partly due to the failure of many women in our society, of all ages and classes, to achieve an episode of sexual release that is of such depth and intensity that there can be no question of what is being experienced. Women are engaging in more sexual activity, premarital and extramarital, but they are not necessarily enjoying it more, if the results of contemporary studies are to be believed (45).

Psychoanalytic theories about the strength of the sex drive and the importance of its gratification, for both men and women, have taken hold in America. But these ideas have yet to become incorporated into the basic image that many women have of themselves as sexual beings. Such women continue to feel guilt and anxiety about a natural human experience that should provoke neither of these emotions.

That Freud gave so much weight to biological factors in the determination of both male and female sexual identity is not remarkable, considering the period during which he wrote and the contemporary state of social scientific knowledge. However, to the extent that psychoanalysis—"the talking cure"—has promoted emphasis on communication and discussion in resolving or reducing conflicts between men and women, it has helped far more than it has hindered authority relations between the sexes.

MALE AND FEMALE LIFE CYCLES. Biological life cycle changes in the human male and female are most dramatic at the extremes—during the early years and toward the end of life. However, sex role changes and conflicts in technologically developed societies are more closely related to values and changing social conditions than they are to biology. This is true for most roles people play.

In highly industrialized societies, the discrepancy between biological and sociological adulthood grows wider. As a rule, individuals are physically mature well before they reach full adulthood legally, politically, and economically. The biological process of aging involves a decline in strength, speed, and agility, as well as diminished acuity of the senses. Often, however, individuals are forcibly retired while still quite able to work.

Under most conditions of work, older employees are not less productive. They compensate for their lessening physical resources by their greater experience and by a stronger commitment to work. Their stronger commitment stems from habit, from lack of realistic alternatives, and from the persistence of the work ethic in our society, at least for the present generation of the aged. At higher occupational levels, employees have greater autonomy and flexibility on their jobs. Professors and business managers do not punch time clocks, and they usually dread retirement unless they are physically ill or severely incapacitated. They are retired to make way for the young, who are more profitable to employ because they start at lower wages or salaries.

This lack of fit between biology and social expectations exists throughout the life cycle. What are these outmoded, contradictory, or unrealistic sex role expectations that persist in our society? In what way are they inappropriate to the biological changes of the male and female life cycle? Viewed generally, the traditional sex role conceptions are equally removed from the biology of the sex life cycle for both sexes; but each sex has its own unique conflicts and frustrations in the various stages of the life cycle. Bear in mind that we are now examining conflicts that are most clearly related to the frustration of biological need and expectations that are incompatible with the biology of the life cycle. Later we turn to sex role conflicts that have little to do with biology.

In infancy and childhood, females tend to have a faster growth rate than males. They mature, on an average, two years earlier than males. Until puberty, girls are often bigger and stronger than boys. Also, it will be recalled, they have greater genetic protection against disease and environmental stress. Conceptions of female fragility and dependence, however, emphasize protection and restriction of strenuous physical activity for female infants and young girls. Girls are held more gingerly as infants, and they are excluded from bodily contact sports with boys. It is probable that the restraint on physical exploratory freedom typically experienced by female children inhibits the individuals' intellectual exploratory capacities in later life. A closed and circumscribed world discourages reaching out, inquiring, and challenging, intellectually, as well as physically.

Sex hormone production increases dramatically for both sexes at puberty, but the heightened sexual drive is repressed in economically stratified societies, particularly for the female. Sexual frustration was much less severe in nonliterate societies, since puberty occurred later, marriage occurred earlier, and premarital sexual freedom was common. Illegitimacy was not a serious problem, however, because puberty and marriage tended to coincide in such societies, and because the human female is not fertile for a period of one to three years after reaching puberty.

In highly industrialized societies, the increased energy which is a biological characteristic of adolescents typically is not channeled into uninhibited sexual gratification or economically productive work activities for either sex. The consequences—in the form of high accident and suicide rates, particularly for male adolescents—are well known.

The discrepancy between sexual drive and sexual gratification differs for men and women in our society throughout the life cycle. Men are most potent and virile in their late teens and early twenties, although psychological factors seem to be very important here. The decline in sexual response of the human male in middle and old age seems to be far more closely related to role expectations and psychological set than to testosterone decline. The "dirty old man" image inhibits the aging male. Nevertheless, in the absence of acute or chronic incapacitating physical illness, males who have been sexually active during their early years can continue "some form of active sexual expression" into their seventies or eighties (46). Most males in our society do not maintain this capacity, for psychological not biological reasons.

Women seldom achieve maximum sexual response capacity until their mid-thirties, very likely because of the more severe sexual repression they experience during childhood and adolescence. Also, pregnancy, if it does not result in obstetrical damage, improves sexual responsiveness. The supply of blood vessels in the pelvic area is permanently increased during and after pregnancy, thus intensifying the engorgement and release experience during orgasm.

The biological aging process does not vary in any major way for the two sexes except insofar as patterns of sex hormone decline differ. Reactions to aging, however, do vary along sex lines. These reactions are very closely related to the differing typical role obligations of the sexes and to cultural values. The decline in energy and strength is a greater source of conflict for the male, whose economic obligations generally do not lighten until retirement (although this decline does not seriously impair the performance of most occupational roles in urbanized, computerized societies). The female, on the other hand, experiences a decline in physical role obligations during the empty-nest stage (when the children are gone), especially if she is not employed. The current trend toward smaller families appears to accentuate this stage, when a woman's problem is likely to be inadequate outlets for physical energies that are still quite strong.

The decline in physical attractiveness that accompanies aging is, or at least has been, a greater source of conflict for females in our society. In our youth-oriented culture, the obvious signs of aging—the atrophying of muscle tissue, the loss of hair pigmentation, and skin, posture, and figure changes, for example—have been more negatively evaluated for the female than for the male. In the entertainment field, males can play romantic leads into their sixties; female actresses are retired much earlier, although character actresses can survive somewhat longer. In most societies, incidentally, physical attractiveness (defined according to varying standards) has been more important for the female than the male (47). This has been particularly true in societies in which women's economic role is of less value than that of the male. Given the increased life span in contemporary societies, as well as the spreading values of companionship, mutual psychological support, and life-long sexual gratification in the husband–wife relationship, this discrepancy in the evaluation of the physical signs of aging has been a greater source of conflict for women.

Hormone changes at childbirth are quite pronounced in women, but here too, the apparent increase in postpartum depression and psychosis (the baby blues) in modern societies seems to be due more to role change and psychological factors than to changes in hormone secretion. With the increasing absence of grandmothers and other relatives to share in the obligations of childrearing in very mobile, industrialized societies, the role of mother becomes more stressful. Young mothers, faced with a complete and never-ending full-time responsibility for another human being, sometimes experience symptoms very like those of battle fatigue in soldiers at the front—a result of exhaustion and the conflicts of a new role for which there has been little adequate preparation (48).

Breast-feeding is also accompanied by distinct hormone changes in the human female; but once again, no significant and consistent relationship has been found between the intensity of maternal feeling and the acceptance or rejection of breast-feeding. Women who do not breast-feed have not been found to be less nurturing toward their young by any measures of this illusive concept that have been used in various studies. In modern society, the decision to breast-feed or not to breast-feed is bound up with the changing, complicated, and often ambiguous demands of the husband–wife relationship. These demands are frequently in conflict with the physical obligations of breast-feeding. If the husband–wife tie is defined as the paramount relationship in the family—as it is, increasingly, in modern nuclear families—a wife will be less apt to take on optional activities that might interfere with her availability to her husband.

Social scientific research and findings have kept pace with these new values and needs: older studies emphasized the oral and emotional deprivation of bottle-feeding relative to breast-feeding; newer studies find no difference in the psychological adjustment of breast-fed or bottle-fed children. A few recent studies, in fact, are beginning to emphasize the negative aspects of breast-feeding. With the continuation of the women's movement in this country, I think we can anticipate an even greater shift in this direction in the scientific literature and in the popular press.

Although the decline in testosterone in the male is gradual and regular throughout the life cycle, beginning at about the age of thirty and continuing until death, the decline in estrogen levels in the female, at menopause, is relatively abrupt. Nevertheless, there is no clear and inevitable relationship between estrogen decline and behavior—sexual or otherwise. Clinical symptoms of menopause vary tremendously among women and within the same woman in relation to changes in her life circumstances which require greater or less physical or mental activity. If she is active and involved, menopausal symptoms are less severe.

Many women, particularly those in the higher income groups, report increased sexual satisfaction after menopause. This effect is very likely related to the disappearance of the fear of pregnancy and to the traveling upward of the fun ethic of the youth counterculture to middle class women, who are more likely to adopt the new values, emphasizing impulse gratification, than are more traditional and more inhibited working class women.

Estrogen replacement therapy does not affect the sexual drive in menopausal women directly, but it may alleviate symptoms of menopause—fatigue, flushing, headaches, pelvic pain—that can inhibit sexual enjoyment. The restoration of estrogen levels also tends to improve the vitality of tissues. This may also improve the sexual response of the aging female indirectly, because of increased morale and improved bodily function. Estrogen therapy does not prevent aging, however, nor does it restore fertility.

BIOLOGY, CULTURE, AND SEX TYPING. Since genetic explanations for the differences in the power and the achievements of the races, the classes, and the sexes are becoming popular once again in America, I felt that it is important to review the material on biological sex differences very carefully and at length. This return to a biological fatalism is probably a reaction to the various liberation movements of the 1960s. It is counterrevolutionary in effect if not in conscious intent. And it may well be a backlash reaction to the civil rights and the women's movements.

Perhaps Americans, with their equalitarian ideology, have tended to ignore biological factors too much, at least within individuals. The idea that biology is destiny is unappealing to achievement-oriented people. But although we are not born equal as individuals, biologically or socially, there is no evidence to establish the existence of different genetically determined "patterns of ability" among the races, classes or sexes, as has been recently claimed. (49).

For example, the phenomenon of "mental shutdown" (the deterioration of intellectual skills and abilities) in adult women cannot be explained as a result of biology. Mental shutdown does not occur in women who experience equal and continuing educational opportunity (50).

In the late nineteenth century, the belief in the innate intellectual inferiority of women found pseudoscientific support in the evolutionary arguments of Herbert Spencer (51). Spencer maintained that since females have faster average growth rates and reach physical maturity earlier than males, they have a less complex and less evolved brain. Therefore, they would have less capacity for abstract reasoning and analysis. This claim has not been substantiated. The belief that biology is more important than environment in determining the abilities of men and women has had many other adherents, however, from Spencer's time right up to the present (52).

But neither human nature nor sexual identity is preordained by biology. To make such a claim is to return to an outmoded ideology stemming from ignorance, self interest, or both. We are not predestined toward any fate—not by our genes, not by original sin, innate depravity, killer instincts, male bonding, or any other concept that has been used, historically and currently, to excuse human irrationality and social injustice.

The appearance of tremendous variations in the behavior and motivations of men and women is the ultimate argument against biological inevitability in the development of the human animal, from birth to death. Genetic, hormonal, and anatomical differences between women and men exist, but for those who fall within the normal range biologically, these differences are irrelevant for most practical and for all humanistic purposes—at least in modern societies.

After a closer look at the typical variations in sex role conceptions and sexual identity within major types of societies, we will have little doubt that technological development and its consequences—direct and indirect, immediate and long-range —provide far better historical explanations of the typical patterns and changes in male and female self conceptions, relationships, and personalities, than biology and biological evolution.

3 | Sexual Identity in Human History

Conceptions of masculinity and femininity have not varied randomly or unpredictably among human societies. This is true also of the degree of sex typing in various societies—the extent of the distinctions that have been made between male and female personalities and activities—and the relative degree of prestige and power of the sexes in different societies. In the three major types of society—nonliterate, agricultural, and industrial —sex-typed role conceptions and the total experience of being born male or female differ in certain typical ways, as do the identities or self conceptions that women and men typically hold.

My division of human societies into the three types is based on the level of their technological development and their state of scientific knowledge (1). If we understand how economic, family, political, educational, and recreational life has varied in nonliterate, agricultural, and industrial societies, we have a basis for explaining the variations in sexual identity that have occurred in human history.

Two major periods of technological innovation have revolutionized social life and male–female relationships. These are the Agricultural Revolution, when the discovery of the technique of plant cultivation occurred, and the Industrial Revolution, when machines were invented to replace manpower. In each period, certain aspects of social life and the male–female relationship underwent gradual, unplanned changes—almost unnoticed while they were occurring, but having a dramatic impact once their ramifications had sunk in.

Material changes are much easier to pinpoint and occur much faster than changes in values, attitudes, and beliefs in human societies. Therefore, as we trace major material changes in human societies, we will notice survivals in the realm of ideas that are no longer appropriate to changed material conditions. Since we are dealing with human beings and individual variability, furthermore, there will be exceptions, reversals, and patterns that do not fit into an orderly scheme. The major trends and variations in sex role conceptions in human societies are clear, however. We can describe them, explain them, and even predict them, within limits.

As we review changing conceptions of masculinity and femininity in human history, we focus mainly on the changing roles men and women have played within family groups. Gender has been the most important basis for assigning rights and obligations and determining the division of labor within the family and within societies. Gender has been a very significant source of differences in the way people are responded to and brought up in human societies.

We will see that conceptions of masculinity and femininity, the degree of sex typing, and the relative prestige and power of the sexes are all interrelated. Where there are extreme sex-typed differences, there will also be extreme differences in the relative power and prestige of the sexes, and conceptions of masculinity and femininity will be most apt to emphasize male aggression and female passivity.

We focus mainly on the changing economic roles of men and women in various types of society to explain sex differences in personality, power, and prestige (2). But this is only one factor, although a most important one. Individuals and the groups to which they belong generally have power—the ability to carry out their will even against resistance (3)—to the extent of their personal as well as their economic resources. Personal resources are intellectual, emotional, and physical—such qualities as intelligence, knowledge, skills, drives, energy, strength, and health. Economic resources are goods—food, land, liquid capital—and the ability to perform services that provide these goods. In sociology and psychology, this view of power is known as the resource theory of power (4).

But resources alone are not enough to account for power differences. People with greater resources do not always claim the power that they could legitimately exercise. Women in the United States own a large percentage of the stocks in large corporations, but they are rarely members of boards of directors. Black women who are more highly educated than their husbands often have less power than their spouses in family life (5).

To understand power relationships, particularly between husband and wife, we must take into account culturally defined values (patriarchalism, for example) which may override the effects of differential resources. But even this factor is not always sufficient to explain the reluctance to claim power that legitimately belongs to certain individuals and groups. As a rule, values change in relation to changing resources; yet discrepancies in behavior often continue long after values have changed. In understanding power relationships between the sexes, we must also apply what one sociologist, Willard Waller, has called "the principle of least interest" (6). This concept was borrowed from an earlier sociologist, E. A. Ross, but Waller made it popular.

Waller claimed that the person who has the least interest in maintaining a relationship can coerce the more interested person into making concessions. For example, black women who are more highly educated than their husbands often do not press claims to greater power because they have more limited alterna-

tives than their husbands; there are relatively few highly educated eligible black males around. Since such women have
fewer alternatives than their husbands, they are more apt to
have a greater interest in maintaining the relationship.

The principle of least interest also applies when we try to understand why, in industrial societies, women with many children
have less power than women with fewer children. Children are
an economic liability in industrial societies. They must spend
long years in school, and they do not contribute to the economic
resources of the family by working in the fields or by otherwise
helping out in family economic enterprises. Having numerous
children to support increases the dependency of the wife and
mother. It limits her alternatives more, since she is not likely to
be able to support these children adequately on her own. Therefore, she would be more invested in maintaining the relationship
with her husband and less apt to lay claim to power that she
might legitimately exercise.

Personal and economic resources, cultural values, and the
principle of least interest, all operate simultaneously in affecting
the man–woman relationship. With this in mind, we can now
try to understand how these factors have affected sexual identity, power, and prestige in nonliterate, agricultural, and industrial societies.

**SEX ROLES IN NONLITERATE, AGRICULTURAL, AND
INDUSTRIAL SOCIETIES.** Humans have lived on earth for
approximately two million years. *Homo sapiens,* the self-pro-
claimed wise man, appeared about 70,000 years ago. The date of
arrival is constantly being pushed back as physical anthropologists discover new fossil remains and improved dating techniques. From the time of the first appearance of humans and
until about 10,000 years ago, when the technique of plant cultivation was discovered, men and women lived as hunters and
gatherers.

Hunting and Gathering Societies. Men, women, and children lived in hunting and gathering societies for about 99 per cent of human history. What were these societies like? To answer this question, we must depend on the archaeological remains of extinct societies and on the studies of hunting and gathering societies that survived into the nineteenth and twentieth centuries. The surviving societies have been observed in Asia, Oceania, and America, in mountain, arctic, desert, or marginal forest areas, where planting is impractical. They were isolated from the currents of change that transformed other societies. Their technology and daily life were probably not identical with their extinct predecessors. We can assume, however, that the political, recreational, economic, religious, and family aspects of these very isolated societies were probably quite similar. These societies changed very slowly and very little through the centuries.

Nonliterate hunting and gathering societies were small (fewer than fifty people, usually). They had no written language. The culture was passed down by oral explanation, cues, and gestures. Most hunting and gathering societies were very mobile, and people moved frequently as local supplies of wild vegetation and game were exhausted. Since there was no economic surplus, all were equal in wealth or poverty. The catch or the kill was shared. All performed most tasks that needed to be done, and seldom were there full-time specialists in any occupation. If there was a shaman or medicine man, he often performed other tasks also. Leaders emerged temporarily in times of decision making, then retired to their daily chores. Tasks were assigned mainly on the basis of age and sex; but lines were not extremely rigid.

Personal qualities such as resourcefulness, intelligence, strength, and health were paramount in determining the prestige and the authority of individuals. Personal property (tools, weapons, clothing) existed but was not accumulated or jealously guarded. Moreover, it could be easily replaced. Ownership of land that was soon to be abandoned was inconceivable; more land was to be had, simply by moving on. The accumulation of liquid capital in the form of shells or other media of exchange was pointless. There was no economic surplus to trade, and there were few handicrafts to exchange among members or with other societies.

Life was short in hunting and gathering societies, but not necessarily brutal or nasty—at least not as a result of human agents. War was unknown. Interlopers were chased off on occasion, but organized warfare of group against group did not exist.

The family performed all major functions—economic, educational, religious, protective, and recreational—and these spheres of life were not separated. There were no teachers, priests, salesmen, police, or full-time entertainers. Family members, interchangeably for the most part, performed all these roles. The nuclear family, consisting of husband, wife, and dependent children, was the basic social unit in most of these societies.

Extended families in which several nuclear families lived together or near one another, exchanging essential services daily and deferring to a common authority, were not common. These are usually a product of more stationary and more technologically developed societies (7).

Nuclear families predominate where people pursue fresh sources of wild vegetation and moving animals or follow the job market. The extended family is too cumbersome to move as a total unit. It is also not likely to exist where life expectancy is short. Three generations usually did not survive long enough to coexist in hunting and gathering societies. As a rule, family relationships were warm in hunting and gathering societies, and the husband—wife relationship was equalitarian. Parent—child relationships were permissive and indulgent. Sex typing was not extreme. Both men and women usually performed economic activities that were equally vital and of equal value. Both sexes were food providers. Women usually gathered plants and hunted small animals. Men—typically bigger, stronger, and faster, and not bound to the hearth by nursing obligations—

pursued larger animals, sometimes for days or weeks at a time.

Although child care was basically a mother's responsibility, all members of the band shared in this task at times—fathers, older siblings—any member who happened to be around when a child needed or wanted something. Cooking was usually done by women, since they stayed closer to the home. But this responsibility might also be assumed by men, depending, again, on who happened to be available.

Leisure time was more abundant than in more technologically developed societies. Anthropologists have estimated that most hunting and gathering societies had the equivalent of a three or four day work week—a goal that contemporary societies are far from achieving. Modern societies have vastly greater productivity levels, but they have far larger populations, and the fruits of technological development are very unequally distributed. Theoretically, if income distribution were equal and all adults worked, a three day work week probably could be achieved once again in human societies.

Leisure activities in hunting and gathering societies were not rigidly sex segregated. All participated actively in singing and dancing. There were usually no secrets exclusive to one sex or the other, no sex-typed esoteric skills, no female deference patterns or other devices that have signified extreme status distinctions between the sexes in more technologically developed societies. The personalities of men and women were not sharply different in hunting and gathering societies. Men were emotionally expressive, as were women. Women were active and assertive, as were men. Men and women did not differ, typically and strongly, in their feelings of self pride and self worth.

Neither families or either of the sexes contributed to, or were able to accumulate, a disproportionate share of the society's economic resources. Women and men were equally dependent on each other for basic subsistence resources. Typically, neither contributed more or less to the family's wealth. The father was not the major provider. The mother was not primarily a food processor rather than a food provider. Therefore, an important source of power difference between men and women in human societies was absent in hunting and gathering societies.

Nonliterate Horticultural Societies.   About 10,000 years ago, the discovery was made—probably by women—that roots could be planted. Since women were the gatherers, they were doubtless the first to notice that stored vegetables or discarded roots, if embedded in soil, could grow again.

This knowledge was accompanied by the invention of the hoe and digging stick in nonliterate horticultural societies. These societies did not have the plow or the knowledge of irrigation, however. They had domesticated animals, but such beasts were a source of food or transportation, rather than power. They did not know how to harness animals to replace manpower in food production.

With the invention of horticulture, social life changed enormously. The status of women and the extent of sex typing also changed, depending largely on the relative value of the economic activities of the sexes in this new type of society.

The technique of plant cultivation and a more dependable food supply made possible a more stationary society. A stationary society meant that extended family forms could more easily develop and be maintained. Clans and tribes became prevalent. An economic surplus was produced, since people grew more than they could consume. This promoted trade, inequality in the resources of families and societies, war, the release of some people to perform more specialized political, religious, economic, and artistic activities, and the invention of other techniques for maintaining or preserving life. Full-time specialized occupations arose when it was no longer necessary for all to be involved in the quest for food. The shaman—skilled in placating or coercing the spirits for the purpose of healing, protecting, or revenging —was one such full-time specialist.

Skills in food preserving techniques, pottery making, and weaving were developed. These early inventions are usually attributed to women, since the techniques involved are associated with tasks generally performed by women in horticultural societies. The decline in the contribution of women to technological development and cultural change is a relatively recent phenomenon in the total span of human history.

The extended family forms that developed more frequently in horticultural societies were either matrilineal (tracing descent through the female line) or patrilineal (tracing descent through the male line). Newlyweds in matrilineal societies usually went to live with the wife's relatives (matrilocal residence). In partrilineal societies, they went to live with the husband's family (patrilocal residence). Usually these descent and residence patterns coincided, and where matrilocal residence patterns existed, the wife's clan was usually in the same village as the husband's clan; thus his family too was nearby. Women, more often, had to go to live among strangers, separated from daily contact with their own relatives, sometimes forever.

Matrilineal and patrilineal family forms tended to exist in relation to the importance of planting, as opposed to hunting, in particular horticultural societies (8). Women, typically, did the planting in horticultural societies. The small gardens were close to home. If planting became relatively more important as a source of food supply, matrilineal family forms tended to develop, and the status of women was higher in such societies. If hunting of large animals or herding was the predominant source of societal wealth, patrilineal forms usually prevailed. In these societies, the status distinctions between the sexes was more extreme. Probably newlywed males remained in their own villages in matrilineal societies at least partly for economic reasons—the men knew the local hunting trails, and a bridegroom would be at a disadvantage if he went to live with his wife's family in another village.

The practice of polygyny (the taking of multiple wives) was

the cultural ideal in a majority of horticultural societies. It tended to occur, however, where women's contribution to the production of food was high. And it was usually limited in extent to wealthier families. The practice of polyandry (the taking of multiple husbands) was very rare, and it occurred where woman's direct contribution to subsistence resources was insignificant. Several husbands (usually brothers) were required to support one woman and her children.

With the invention of horticulture, sex typing became more extreme and the division of labor between the sexes more rigid (9). The double standard came into existence, although it was not universal by any means. It was usually applied more stringently to girls and women of wealthier clans or families. Boys and girls were separated early and prepared for different initiation rites. The folklore that was passed down during the period of preparation for initiation differed for the two sexes and was regarded as the privileged and secret possession of each sex. Recreational activities became increasingly sex-segregated, and the separation of the sexes, generally, increased.

The menstrual taboo became widespread. Women were sometimes secluded and isolated during menstruation. In some societies, they were forbidden while menstruating to cook for males, to touch their tools or weapons, or to participate in religious ceremonies. The strength of these taboos and the restrictions against women during menstruation seems to have been related to the degree of power differences between the sexes in various societies (10). And this, in turn, has tended to be closely related to the economic roles of the sexes.

Elaborate, sex-typed patterns of dress, adornment, and body scarification became one way of validating the difference in the relative status of the sexes. Generally, and despite exceptions, in societies where extreme achievement differences have been emphasized for males as opposed to females, females have been more elaborately adorned. People validate status typically by real achievements or by adornment and dress.

Typical personality differences between the sexes also become more extreme as societies develop technologically. One investigator has described the phenomenon as follows:

> The cross-cultural mode is that males are more sexually active, more dominant, more deferred to, less responsible, less nurturant and less emotionally expressive than females. The extent of these differences varies by culture. And in some cultures, some of these differences do not exist (and occasionally the trend is actually reversed). These differences are related to and presumably influenced by which sex controls economic capital, the extent and kind of division of labor by sex, the degree of political "authoritarianism," and family composition (11).

The last-mentioned factors are all interrelated and are ultimately related to the level of technological development. Extreme sex differences in socially defined identity and personality traits, which occur as societies develop technologically, have been particularly prevalent in societies that hunt large animals or tend herds (12). This feature is a spin-off from the typical differences in strength and reproductive roles between the sexes. Herding and hunting large animals requires greater strength than cultivating gardens and involves wandering greater distances from home.

The increasing prevalence of the extended family in horticultural societies also reinforced greater sex typing. Same-sex substitutes were readily available to take over the activities of a wife or husband who was incapacitated. If a mother was ill, the husband did not have to assume homemaking or childrearing duties. Grandmothers, aunts, and older female children took over. In contrast, among relatively isolated nuclear families of modern societies, if the wife goes into the hospital to bear another child, for example, the husband stays home with the other children (13). Rigid sex typing is less easily maintained.

Agricultural Societies. Agricultural societies appeared about 5,000 years ago in Egypt and Mesopotamia. Technologically, they differed from horticultural societies primarily in their use of the plow, their knowledge of irrigation, and their techniques for harnessing domestic animals as an additional source of power.

Certain characteristics that distinguish horticultural from hunting and gathering societies became even more pronounced in early agricultural societies. The economic surplus was greater, the number of specialized occupations grew, economic inequality between families and societies became more pronounced, the size and permanence of settlements increased (urban centers were common), wars of conquest, subjugation, and occupation became common, and the status of women declined, for the most part, and in most agricultural societies.

Agricultural societies developed a written language, probably in response to the need to keep records of taxes collected from conquered territories. They developed sizable bureaucracies—organizations that coordinate the activities of many people in the carrying out of large-scale tasks. Military bureaucracies were established to handle the task of empire building and maintenance. Religious bureaucracies arose to cope with the problem of spiritual control of diverse populations with different cultures (14).

Theologies contained systems of ethics and conceptions of morality based ultimately on supernatural sanctions. Believers were united into moral communities led by members of the richest and most powerful families. These families also supplied the personnel for political leadership. Hence the phenomenon of theocracy arose.

Polygamy, the cultural ideal in a majority of the nonliterate societies for which we have information, was replaced by monogamy. Monogamy probably became nearly universal in response to the changed economic roles of women in agricultural societies. Women's subsistence economic activities declined dramati-

cally in value relative to those of males. Women became largely
food processors. They became more dependent on men, and to
support more than one wife became more difficult for most men.
Men, however, particularly in richer families, were less restricted to monogamous sexual relationships than women. Prostitutes, concubines, slaves, and female members of poorer families provided additional sexual outlets for relatively wealthy
males.

Patrilineal and patriarchal family forms became the norm in
agricultural societies. This is understandable if we remember
that women in matrilineal societies tended to have very important economic roles. They were the planters, and they sometimes contributed more economic resources to the family than
men—particularly when hunting was not important. If resources
are more unequally contributed, and if the male contributes
more of the basic economic resources than the female, patrilineal and patriarchal family forms become prevalent.

The more extreme sex typing and the greater relative power
of males in most agricultural societies do not rest entirely or ultimately on differences in their economic resources, however.
Ultimately, economic activities in agricultural societies, as in
nonliterate societies, are determined by the different biological
resources of the sexes in reproduction, as well as in size and
strength. Males have contributed relatively more to economic
resources in societies requiring the herding of large animals, the
felling of large trees, the bailing of hay, and the plowing and
tending of distant fields. Most males are better equipped biolog
ically to perform such chores, and they have not been restricted
to the home by nursing obligations.

In agricultural societies, the extreme distinctions in the status,
power, and personalities of the sexes have been mitigated by
class. One historian, Mary Beard, has argued that historically
the subjection of women has been a matter of class rather than
gender (15). She points to the very high status and power that
royal and aristocratic women have had, for example, in medie-

val society. Certainly it was higher relative to lower status males. Nevertheless, aristocratic women did not have equal or greater power than their husbands, particularly when they were not permitted to control their inheritances. And women as a group, no matter what their status, have never controlled entire societies. Queens were and are surrounded by male, not female, advisors. Here, again, I think we must look to the ultimate basis of power: the personal resources of physical size and strength which, if closely related to the requirements of economic activities—as they are in technologically less developed societies—strongly affect the relative power of the sexes.

With the development of agriculture, the tendency for women and men to evaluate themselves as inferior or superior on the basis of gender became even more pronounced than it had been in horticultural societies. In many agricultural societies the negative self conceptions of women were reinforced by theologies that proclaimed the inferiority of women and prescribed male dominance as natural law.

Owing to differences in climate, geography, cultural values, the fortunes of war, and other idiosyncratic factors, technological development proceeded unevenly in different agricultural societies. Most eventually learned to harness wind and water power, and some, in the West, initially, replaced manpower with machine power.

Industrial Societies. The beginning of the Industrial Revolution is usually traced to England in the eighteenth century. The discovery of the use of water power to drive machines, and later, electric power, atomic power (and probably, solar energy eventually), has had tremendous consequences for social life and for the typical activities, identities, and relationships of men and women.

We could list thousands of changes that have occurred in family life, and in economic, political, religious, and recreational life, over the past 200 years since societies began to industrialize. But some changes have been more significant than others for male and female consciousness, personality, power, and privilege. It is these changes that need to be analyzed particularly.

World population has increased almost sixfold in the past two centuries. Traditional societies (nonliterate and agricultural) were characterized by high birthrates and high death rates. The advances in scientific medicine that accompanied industrialization have lowered the death rate and at least doubled the average life span. Scientific advances also promoted a lower birthrate, once values began to change in the direction of small as opposed to big families—at least in highly industrialized societies. In industrializing nations, the dramatic lowering of the death rate has resulted in what has been called the "population explosion." High birthrates continue because values change more slowly than circumstances.

The increase in population, the diminished need for manpower in an industrial economy where machines do a great deal of the work, the fact that most children who are born reach adulthood, and the need to train these children for many years to function in technologically complex societies—all these factors have operated to devalue woman's role as childbearer. Fertility continues to define femininity and masculine virility in industrializing countries, but not as much as in the past.

In traditional societies, barren women were viewed as cursed. The young hunters and the gatherers, the field hands, and the warriors and rulers that women produced added to family resources. In modern societies, children are an economic burden, as are the aged. Both are outside the productive process—unable to participate in the corporate economy and unnecessary for the creation of wealth within nations and within families.

In very modern societies, some women, a handful to be sure, are voluntarily barren. In the United States today, organizations of childless couples (who call themselves "child free") exist to provide social support and reinforcement for the choice of a childless existence.

Governments institute family allowance programs to encourage the birthrate in more technologically developed societies. Children are borne primarily for psychological reasons—emotional gratification, companionship, love. Couples can choose not to have children if they feel that they are not psychologically equipped for the experience, or if they feel no need to have children. And those who do reproduce are more apt to question their choice—at least at times, and particularly within certain less traditional segments of the society.

The lengthened life span also has important implications for sex role conceptions and behavior. At the turn of the century, parents rarely lived to see all their children grown and married. Now the average couple, with an average number of children who were born at the usual time in the life cycle, will spend at least fifteen years together after the children have left the home. And here, too, new values define the relationship. Love, psychological support, friendship, companionship, and erotic gratification are the standards, increasingly, for maintaining the husband–wife relationship in modern societies.

The traditional standards of physical survival and economic cooperation are less pressing when the standard of living rises and when more economic alternatives exist for women as well as for men. As factories and corporations replace the family as the basic economic productive unit in highly industrialized societies, women are gradually drawn into the industrial economy, particularly before and after the childbearing and childrearing years. In the United States in the 1900s, the typical woman worker was in her twenties and unmarried. The American typical woman worker in the 1970s is married and in her forties or fifties (16). All her children are grown and have left home. She and her husband are in a stage of the family life cycle that sociologists have dubbed "the empty nest." And, if she is out working, she is once again contributing to the basic economic resources of the family. She becomes an economic provider as well as a consumer, household manager, and worker. Tasks such as weaving, spinning, food preserving, and preparing have been assumed by factories and corporations, and woman's loss of status that is largely derived, historically, from the declining value of her services as childbearer and processor of raw materials, increases as does her relative power in family life.

Married women who work have more authority in the family than those who do not work (17). The longer they work, the more authority they have. They have higher self esteem, typically, than women who do not work. And if they outearn their husbands, they tend to become dominant in their relationship with their husbands (18).

As societies develop technologically, jobs in extractive and manufacturing industries (farming, fishing, lumbering, mining, and factory jobs) decline in number relative to distributing, selling, technical, and professional jobs. The differences in average size and strength between the sexes becomes less significant in determining economic activities, and economic opportunities for women increase dramatically. According to the 1970 United States census, for example, close to four million new jobs were created during the 1960s. This work was mainly in nonmanual fields, and women took almost two-thirds of these jobs (19).

To work in an industrial economy, particularly at the middle levels of occupational skills, women must be literate. As societies develop technologically, women become more highly educated, and the gap between men and women in this particular resource begins to close. In the working class in the United States, in fact, women are apt to be more educated than their husbands, since they are less likely to drop out of high school. Education becomes another resource that raises the status of women in complex, literate societies.

Sex typing also declines somewhat as the qualities of personality (e.g., assertiveness, resourcefulness, independence, achievement motivation) that are required for employment in the corporate economy become essential for women as well as for men. Parents, in bringing up their children, emphasize values that will equip their children to function adequately as adults. If their female children are likely to work at gainful occupations at least part of their lives (and this becomes almost universal in highly industrialized societies), parents will emphasize traits of personality that will better equip both their daughters and their sons to earn their livings as adults.

In computerized and automating economies, however, most working women continue to find employment in sex-typed occupations. They are overwhelmingly concentrated in occupations clearly related to traditional female sex role activities and personality traits—canning and clothing factories, teaching, nursing, social work, dietetics—and at occupational levels that require little in the way of authority or leadership qualities. Because of the continued sex typing of most occupations (even in the Scandinavian countries, where official government policy has been directed toward breaking down sex typing), there is little real competition for jobs between men and women at the lower occupational levels.

The number of unemployed men does not begin to equal the number of women employed in industrial economies. And if all women were removed from the economy, the male unemployment rate would be little affected. Few unemployed males would take jobs as secretaries, nurses, or sales persons in women's underwear departments. Women become essential and irreplaceable in occupations outside the family in highly developed economies. Their relative status rises again, approaching the high status of women in many nonliterate societies.

At the same time, other factors operate to break down sex typing in modern societies. Mobility is most important in this respect. People move socially—up and down in the class structure. They move geographically—in response to the push and pull of the changing job market. And they are mobile psychologically. They identify with many more models and with models who are not in their immediate environments.

As women move away from their extended families, role segregation within the nuclear family breaks down further. Marriage across class, religious, and racial lines, which becomes
more common in industrial societies, also promotes the breakdown of ties with extended families. Class differences between
the generations, particularly as younger generations are more
highly educated, also fosters the independence of the nuclear
family. Husband and wife become increasingly interdependent.
The isolated nuclear family is not typical, by any means, in the
United States, but it is becoming more frequent, especially in
the middle classes. Husbands in the middle class are apt to be
more actively involved in household and childrearing activities,
since grandmothers, sisters, and aunts are less readily available to maintain the sexual division of labor than in the working class.

The mass media present mainly sex-typed images of female
and male personality and behavior. But more and more nontra-
ditional role models are now available—women's movement
leaders, female politicians, scientists, lawyers, doctors, jockeys,
and baseball catchers. Such models are rare, but they do appear
in the media more frequently than in the past. And they can expand psychological horizons for their contemporaries in a way
that was impossible in the days of the isolated, illiterate, house-
bound rural wife and mother.

Today in America adult, married women play one of three
major roles. They are traditional wives and mothers. They are
hostesses and companions to their husbands. Or they play the
partner role (20). These roles are not mutually exclusive. What I
am describing is the relative emphasis and the major focus of
the relationship between husbands and wives.

Ideally, the woman who plays the traditional role in her home
has the right to security, support, alimony in the case of divorce,
respect as a wife and mother, loyalty and fidelity of the husband
for whom she has borne children and provided nurturing ser-

vices, and gratitude for services performed for husband and children. She is obliged to bear and rear children, to perform domestic services, and to subordinate her own interests to the economic plans of her husband. She must accept a limited and restricted range of interests and activities, at least during the childrearing stage of her marriage.

The companion role is typical in the upper class, although it occurs in the middle class in combination with the traditional role, particularly during the empty nest stage of the marriage. In this kind of relationship, important rights of the wife include the sharing of recreational activities with the husband, erotic gratification and romantic response, ample funds for dress and recreation, freedom from housework and childrearing chores, and chivalrous treatment by the husband. The wife's obligations include the management of servants and nurses, the preservation of physical attractiveness at the risk of marital insecurity (the relationship is not reinforced by the rendering of essential domestic services), being alert, stimulating, and interesting, and cultivating and maintaining important social contacts for the husband.

Married women who play the partner role are gainfully employed and make important contributions to family economic resources. Ideally, they are economically independent, exercise equal authority in the family, are exempt from one-sided domestic service to the husband, and have equal freedom to pursue nonfamily interests—occupational, friendship, political, and recreational. Insofar as they are able, they are required to contribute to the economic support of the children and to household expenses. They do not claim alimony in the event of a divorce.

The traditional role is still the most prevalent in American society. Approximately 60 per cent of the married women in America play this role, full time, and it is still defined as the feminine ideal by a majority of the population. The companion role is increasingly valued in all segments of our society, and some variant of this role is played by growing numbers of women, depending on income, leisure, education, and class.

The partner role is increasing, although even professional women, who would most closely approach the ideal in this kind of relationship, continue to assume ultimate and disproportionate responsibility for homemaking and childrearing (21). They are junior partners, at best, in the current scramble for equality (22). Husbands continue to be the major, if not the sole provider, in the great majority of families. Only 3 per cent of American women who are employed full time earn more than 10,000 dollars a year (23).

Women will not be able to achieve full equality in their relationships with their husbands until they have equal resources—economic, educational, and psychological. They have much more authority, at least in routine decision-making, than they had, typically, in agricultural societies. But the husband usually prevails in areas of major conflict within the family—a dispute over when or whether to move in response to a new job opportunity, for example.

Actually, perfect equality in decision-making powers between husband and wife would often lead to a stalemate. More and more frequently, in highly industrial societies, however, traditional values, emphasizing male dominance, decline at the same time that women's resources increase. A situational exercise of power occurs more often. Marital partners who prevail in a marriage that is defined as equalitarian prevail only at certain times and under certain circumstances. They prevail because they are more invested in a decision or more competent in terms of resources to make the decision.

Rapid social change breaks down rigid cultural traditions. The growth of higher level jobs requires more flexibility, autonomy, and independence in the job situation in modern societies. Females as well as males, at least within the upper, more mobile classes, are reared more permissively. The permissive ideal is one in which the child's individual and unique needs are taken into account in teaching and disciplining. This applies whether the child is male or female. Infants are not fed on arbitrary four hour schedules. Smaller infants are fed more frequently, and there is a growing trend to feed all infants on demand, according to their individual needs.

To raise children to obey rules unquestioningly is inappropriate if their life circumstances will be characterized by constant social change. The rules will be constantly changing or they will be nonexistent. Modern men and women have to be resourceful and independent. Girls as well as boys are subject to these changed parental expectations, increasingly. But sex typing is still strong, even in America, which is by far the most mobile and the most technologically advanced country in the world.

Nevertheless, of particular significance for sexual identity are certain conditions that become prevalent in industrial societies—lower birthrates, longer life spans, the expansion in the number of nonmanual occupations, increasing employment and educational opportunities for women, very rapid social change, the breakdown of traditional values, and the spread of permissive childrearing practices. These conditions directly promote less rigid conceptions of masculinity and femininity. Women become more aggressive. Men become more emotionally expressive. The status of women rises, their self conceptions become more positive, and the relationship between the sexes becomes somewhat more equalitarian.

Once again, in modern times as in the earliest stages of technological development, more women are permitted to make major discoveries and contributions to the culture—discoveries that must now be made largely in the nonfamily occupational world. The process of psychological liberation for women is slower than political or economic liberation, but it is inevitable, given the conditions that promote it. Waste has become a problem in technologically developed societies—the waste of women's talents no less than other kinds of waste.

THE HISTORICAL TREND. In discussing variations in sexual identity in major types of societies, the historical picture has emerged, in very broad dimensions. A closer look, however, indicates that despite exceptions and human variability, the explanations that I have offered for the changing collective fate of most men and women in human history are generally valid. In referring to traditional patterns that are changing, I use the past tense for describing historical male–female relationships and identities in various societies. But social change is slower in industrializing nations than in automated and computerized nations. What was true in the past is still very largely true for many countries in the present, particularly in rural areas.

Although the status of women declined, for the most part, in agricultural societies, local circumstances—religious, philosophic, or political ideologies, geography, natural resources, climate, and war and conquest, for example have made for local and temporary variations in the status and self conceptions of women within various agricultural societies.

Sex Roles in the West. In ancient Minoan civilization, women worked in the fields beside their men (24). The separation of the sexes was minimal in all areas of life. Privilege and prestige were more equally distributed between the sexes. The typical symbols of the low status of women were absent: extreme sex typing, seclusion, veiling, and female-to-male deference patterns. Ancient Crete was characterized by goddess-worshipping cults, as were the high civilizations of Egypt and Mesopotamia. These cults exalted certain characteristics of the female, an attitude that promoted and reflected a somewhat higher status of women in daily life.

On mainland Greece, among the Mycenaeans and Acheans, woman's economic role deteriorated relative to that of the male. Fighting and hunting were more significant for the fate of the society. The sexes were more segregated in terms of activities, communication, and recreation, although not to the same extent as in classical Greece.

The Spartans were characterized by an intermediate pattern. The military state, after the Dorian conquest, valued male warriors above all, but the values of stoicism, self reliance, and resourcefulness applied to women also. Spartan women were assertive, independent, and relatively unconfined within the family, as compared with the typical patriarchal pattern in other agricultural societies.

The very low status of women in democratic Athens is a historical puzzle that has not been satisfactorily explained. Women in classical Athens were legally without power. They could be sold into concubinage by their fathers or brothers. Wealthier women were completely segregated—confined to special quarters at the rear of the house. They could appear outdoors (outside the immediate neighborhood) only if heavily veiled and escorted by attendants. And they appeared outdoors only for very special occasions—weddings, funerals, and religious or theatrical events (25). Greek men of high social rank turned to courtesans—the educated, witty, and gifted heterae—and to other men for intellectual and sexual gratification. Greek wives, limited and illiterate, were uninteresting and uninspiring.

Possibly the low status of women during the classical period in Greece represented a scapegoat reaction on the part of aristocratic Greek males, who themselves experienced a loss of status with the establishment of Greek democracy (26). Historically, women and other weaker groups have often served as scapegoats when males have lost status, wars, or property, or when they have experienced other serious economic, political, or sexual frustrations.

Another possible explanation, even more psychological in emphasis, is that Greek male oppression of women was a reaction formation to male fear of the Greek mother, who was all-powerful within the home. Because of extreme sex typing, Greek males

were under virtually complete domination of the mother during
the early formative years of their lives:

> The social position of women and the psychological influ-
> ence of women are thus quite separate matters. The
> Greek male's contempt for women was not only compati-
> ble, but indissolubly bound to an intense fear of them and
> to an underlying suspicion of male inferiority. Why else
> would such extreme measures be necessary? Customs
> such as the rule that a woman should not be older than
> her husband, or of a higher social status, or more edu-
> cated, or paid the same as a male for the same work, or
> be in a position of authority—betray an assumption that
> males are incapable of competing with females on an
> equal basis; the cards must first be stacked, the male
> given a handicap (27).

These are interesting explanations, but economic factors were
also very relevant. The well-to-do Greek wife played the role of
household manager, completely dependent on her husband, as
she had been previously on her father. Poor Athenian women,
who went out to work and contributed directly to the economic
resources of their families, shared a rough equality with their
husbands—in classical Greece and throughout history.

In Republican Rome the legal rights of women were also very
limited. Women and children were regarded as the property of
the male head of the household. Wealthier women of the Roman
republic were educated, however, at least through the elementary school level. Husbands and wives dined together and
shared other activities to a greater extent than in Athens.

The legal status of women did not change much during the
era of the Roman Empire, but their actual status changed
greatly. During the long periods of absence of the empire-build-
ing males, Roman wives managed property, made decisions, and
developed competence and self confidence in handling family
economic affairs. It is an irony of history that where sex typing
is extreme, war is more prevalent. But when men are away at

war, the status and power of women rises and sex typing declines.

In the early period of the empire, finishing schools appeared for upper class Roman women, emphasizing primarily the arts. Toward the end, women were entering many higher status occupations, although not without difficulty. Among the poor, the growth of urban centers encouraged outside employment of women in factory work and in trade, thus enhancing their status also.

During the Middle Ages, under the sway of Christian religious ideology, women experienced a decline in status relative to imperial Rome. St. Paul, possibly in response to the general licentiousness of the upper classes in Rome, had enunciated the ideals of sexual abstinence and the subjection of women: "For a man indeed aught not to have his head veiled, forasmuch as he is the image and glory of God: but the woman is the glory of the man: for neither was the man created for the woman but the woman for the man: for this cause aught the woman to have a sign of authority on her head" (28).

At best, the attitude of the early Christians toward women was ambivalent: woman, as the wife of Adam, was the temptress and the instrument of man's loss of innocence. As the mother of Christ, however, she was pure and undefiled. This ambivalence was reflected in the structure of the medieval church. Usually subordinate to the priestly hierarchy, nuns were often permitted the exercise of vast authority and leadership within the confines of the convent.

The status of women during the Middle Ages varied, particularly in relation to wars and the absence of males. During the period of the crusades, for example, aristocratic women managed estates, stood siege, assumed certain political functions, and otherwise enjoyed privileges and power denied to males of lower status. At the middle levels, in urban centers, many women were employed directly in economic enterprises, although the guilds limited their access to training within various crafts and in the professions.

The pattern of chivalry and romantic love in the man–woman relationship arose in the twelfth century among the upper classes in Europe (29). The aristocratic woman was idealized, as was her knightly love. But arranged marriages prevailed, since the authority of the land-based aristocratic family was still very great. Romantic or courtly love occurred outside marriage, and such relationships were usually not consummated sexually. Christian doctrine, emphasizing abstinence, continued to be very effective.

The pedestal phenomenon, in which women are idealized and extremely protected and dependent, appeared also in the southern regions of the United States during the colonial era. Survivals of this pattern are still found in the South. This idealization of women did little to enhance their actual power or their conceptions of themselves as competent, capable human beings in the southern states, any more than in medieval Europe, however. Sex typing continued to be extreme, except during exceptional circumstances (wars, usually), and then only temporarily.

Wealthier women shared in the temporary freeing of the creative and the erotic impulse during the Renaissance in Europe. Many upper class women participated in the revival of the arts and of learning. Salons, operated by women and promoting lively intellectual exchange between educated adults, spread from Italy throughout most of Europe during the Renaissance. Since arranged marriage continued to be the custom, extramarital outlets became more frequent, in a climate of psychological liberation. Prostitutes, courtesans, and noncommercial liaisons flourished at all social levels. Women, too, shared in this liberation, but only a small number and in a very limited way.

During the early stages of capitalism in the West, women generally experienced a further decline in status. Initially, the rise of the urban middle classes promoted sexual equality and diminished sex typing. Middle class women worked in trade and often played the partner role, although basically still within the patriarchal setting. With the removal, under the factory system, of many economic productive functions from the family, the economic contribution of middle class women declined. Their virtual exclusion from higher education closed off avenues of occupational achievement to them. Working class women fared even worse. They were brutally exploited as a source of cheap labor.

Gainful employment for middle class women came to be defined as degrading and unfeminine. In later stages of industrialization, however, the same middle classes were the first to emphasize higher education for their daughters as well as their sons. Given inheritance taxes and the insecurities accompanying rapid change, education became a major value in the parental search for security for their female as well as their male children.

In America, from the beginning, rigid sex typing and extreme differences in the power and prestige of the sexes were mitigated by special circumstances. Among the most important factors promoting greater equality between the sexes were the shortage of women, the mobility encouraged by the frontier—extended families were not common in the United States until after the massive European immigration of the nineteenth and early twentieth centuries, if then (30)—and the individualism of restless, independent immigrants and pioneers. The American dream embraced women, too, to some extent, particularly in the newer areas of the western United States.

Conceptions of masculinity and femininity and the relative status of the sexes varied greatly in the colonies in relation to local conditions and dominant religious theologies (31). The widespread shortage of women led to a modification in the practices, originally brought over from England, of arranged marriage and the dowry. Young men and women generally chose their own partners, although as a rule marriages could not take place without parental consent.

Economic considerations were not irrelevant even in self-chosen arrangements. Young people could and often were as expedient as their elders would have been in selecting marital prospects. Regardless of how the choice was made, however, young women could not be pressured into marrying without their consent—a right that was not usually granted to women in other, strongly patriarchal societies.

The laws in colonial America also reflected the somewhat higher status and independence of women. Men were forbidden by law to beat their wives. And although a wife could not own property unless it was given to her by her husband, she could gain control of property when her husband died. In the South and in the Middle Atlantic colonies, furthermore, women could legally own land in their own names.

In the New England colonies, patriarchal doctrines embodied in the Puritan religion defined women as inferior and dangerously carnal. A life circumscribed by home and church was the ideal—an ideal often mitigated in practice by the requirements of active participation in economic production.

In the West, under conditions of extreme hardship, pioneer women developed characteristics of independence, resourcefulness, competence, and self pride. Sex typing declined as mutuality and equality were promoted by the isolation and total economic interdependence of nuclear family members.

In the South, on the other hand, the mild and generous climate, the more tolerant attitude of the Church of England toward women, an even greater shortage of women than in the East, and the existence of a servant and slave class, promoted a chivalrous idealization of wealthier women—the pedestal phenomenon. This circumstance had few practical consequences for power relationships between the sexes, however, since dependence is not a resource that promotes equality.

The absence of a tradition of viewing women as temptresses and as instruments of the devil in the South protected them from the witch hunts of the New England colonies. At the same time, however, the view of women as pure and spiritual encouraged wealthier males to seek sexual gratification from slaves, servants, and other, presumably more earthy women.

Sex Roles in the East. Historically, the degree of sex typing, the strength of feelings of female inferiority and powerlessness, and the inequality in the status of men and women were far more extreme in the East than in the West. In the East, characterized by late industrialization and slow rates of social change, the religious and philosophical ideologies of the Orient, which stressed the inferiority of women, held sway longer and operated more effectively.

In China, for example, Confucian philosophy, emphasizing extreme hierarchical status distinctions between elders and the young (filial piety) and between male and female, reinforced the subordinate status of women (32). Practices symbolizing this inferior status included female infanticide, concubinage, female slavery, and foot-binding (which crippled and hampered the physical mobility and freedom of upper status women). Ancestor worship, which was the responsibility of the first-born male heir, promoted a commodity view of women as bearers of sons. With rare exceptions, women were illiterate in a society in which learning was exalted and political leadership was determined by the mastery of an elaborate system of ideographs and the ability to pass examinations on the Confucian classics.

The extended family and clan, as ideal and as actuality, was more prevalent than in the West, although probably multigenerational households were not typical even in China, particularly among the poor. A household consisting of the eldest son, his parents, wife, and children, appears to have been the closest to the ideal that most families were able to attain—and then, often, only during the early years of the son's marriage. But members of extended families did tend to live near one another, if not in the same household. They did, then, exchange services daily and depend on one another. It is this type of extended family structure that has probably been most prevalent in almost all traditional societies.

The practice of patrilocal residence in a society emphasizing filial obedience and the primacy of the parent–child tie over the husband–wife relationship made for severe hardship for the young Chinese bride. Since marriages were arranged and usually took place between young people from different villages, the young bride lived among strangers—including her husband, unless she had been sold to the husband's family at an early age. Living under the total domination of her mother-in-law, she could do little to raise her status until she produced a son. She could not achieve any degree of real authority within the family until she herself became a mother-in-law. This prospect undoubtedly kept many women in line, under what might otherwise have been unbearable conditions.

Among the most important traditional grounds for divorce in China were barrenness and disobedience to the husband's parents. Custody of the children, incidentally, was usually awarded to the husband and his family. If the wife found her situation intolerable in her mother-in-law's home, she had little recourse. Suicide was not uncommon in traditional China, although the extent of this practice has probably been exaggerated (33).

The emphasis on the parent–child rather than the husband–wife relationship, as well as the extreme status differences between men and women, promoted warm affectional ties and the seeking of psychological gratification between women and their children. This pattern was typical in patriarchal, agricultural societies. It persists in modern societies among more traditional elements of the population.

Girls in traditional China were brought up to obey males: in childhood, their fathers, in adulthood, their husbands, and in middle and old age, if they were widowed, their grown sons. Although superficially passive, at least in wealthier families, Chinese women have often been portrayed in the folklore as having inordinate strength and courage. This would seem to be appropriate, given the hardships of daily life.

Peasant women in traditional China were certainly strong and had a somewhat higher status, in relation to their husbands, than wealthier women. Their services in economic production were essential. They were less likely to be locked into a large extended family, since resources to support this structure were lacking. Their husbands were less likely to take concubines, since they couldn't afford them. And peasant women were unlikely to have had their feet bound, since they would be unable to work, if crippled.

Similar patterns in the male–female relationship existed also in traditional Japan (34). Here too, rigid roles and status distinctions were based on age and sex. Unlike China, Japan has always faced a shortage of land, and this has prevented equal inheritance among all sons. The three-generational extended household, therefore, was not likely to include more than the parents, the oldest son, his wife and children, and his unmarried siblings. Other patterns were quite similar to those in China, however—arranged marriage, the double standard, patrilocal residence, concubinage, and female infanticide. Nevertheless, there seems to have been somewhat more consideration for the rights of young people and of women. Young unmarried men and women were usually allowed to meet before marriage arrangements were concluded by their families, and their consent and approval were sought. Romantic love themes have a long history in Japanese classical literature.

As elsewhere, the status of women in traditional Japan varied according to the individual's economic role. Working class and peasant women tended to have more advantages in this respect than did well-to-do women. The dominant wife is another theme that runs through the traditional folklore.

In Japanese fishing villages, women were directly involved in subsistence economic activities. They did the farm work, and they sometimes fished. In mountain areas, where men engaged in forestry, women did the farming. Women were also silk producers, until the silk textile industry became mechanized and was moved to urban areas. In farming villages, on the other hand, women's work did not involve major contributions to subsistence, and their status was lower.

As in other patriarchal, agricultural societies, seclusion and separation symbolized the inferior status of women in traditional Japan. Women walked, ate, slept, and socialized separately; their inferiority was also signified by silence or lowered voice, averted gaze, and humility and self sacrifice, rather than pride and self indulgence.

Yet self control and constraint, particularly of aggressive impulses, was and is a central aspect of both the masculine and the feminine ideal personalities in Japan. This personality trait was not sex-typed historically, nor was the need to achieve. Both sexes felt a strong need to excel according to the culturally defined standards of excellence, whether in economic activities, homemaking, or childbearing. Both felt a strong responsibility to fulfill prescribed obligations, whatever these might be. And both felt intense shame at obvious failure to fulfill the expectations of others. Men and women deferred ritualistically to superior authority, whatever the basis of this authority—age, sex, wealth, or political power.

In traditional India, the Hindu religion promoted a very fatalistic, otherworldly orientation, promising rewards in later incarnations to compensate for inferior status and other miseries experienced in this world (35). The caste system also reinforced status differences between the sexes, lowering geographic mobility and discouraging the utilization of women (and men) in the recruitment to the new economic and educational positions that became available with incipient industrialization. The Indian population is still largely illiterate and, as in other countries, far higher percentages of women than men cannot read or write.

The desire to maintain caste lines promoted the practice of arranged marriage in India. Another factor was added that restricted free choice and facilitated family control over marriage. The customs of purdah (the seclusion of women) and child marriage (before or at the beginning of puberty) also increased family authority in arranging marriages and enhanced male authority in the home. Usually a very young girl, or infant, was betrothed to an older male. A young, inexperienced, and uneducated bride was easier to control.

The Hindu religion, in which women were viewed as strongly erotic and as potential subverters of male asceticism and spirituality, reinforced the practices of seclusion and separation of women. Hidden behind the veil and in voluminous garments, young girls and women were never seen by men who were not members of their immediate families.

The dowry system also restricted the freedom of choice of young women. Where women played a direct role in economic production (e.g., in horticultural societies), the practice of bride price, paid by the groom's family, tended to be prevalent. The bride's family was compensated for the loss of a productive worker. Since the bride price was not returnable in the event of divorce, this custom promoted somewhat better treatment of the wife. The position of women was somewhat enhanced by the potential loss of resources by the husband and his family if the wife returned to her home. The dowry system prevailed in societies where women's economic role centered around ancillary activities—processing and preparing raw materials provided by males—or in the upper classes, where she functioned mainly as childbearer and household manager.

Among the untouchable castes in traditional India, the groom paid a bride price. Its size depended on the bride's status on entering the marriage—virgin, widowed, or divorced—and according to whether and how many additional productive workers (children) she brought into the marriage. Among the higher castes, dowries were provided by the bride's family. Usually the size of the dowry varied with the relative statuses of the families involved. The families of brides provided larger dowries if the bride married upward in the social scale or if she was unattractive.

Divorce and the remarriage of widows were permitted among the lower castes but were prohibited to upper caste women. The practice of *sati*—the burning of upper caste widows upon the death of their husbands—guaranteed fidelity to dead husbands. Males could remarry, however, even though the Hindu religion prescribed the reunion of the souls of husband and wife after death. The remarried widower, presumably, would find himself in a polygynous situation after death.

Polygyny was infrequent in Hindu society, and as in other societies, it was practiced mainly by rich and powerful men. Polyandry occurred in areas that were not predominantly Hindu —among the Todas of southern India, for example. Toda society was characterized by a sexual division of labor in which women performed few functions that directly contributed to the wealth of the family.

The joint family—all adult males and their wives and children living with the parents under one roof—was the ideal in most of traditional India, as it was in China. But here too, as in China, the extended family ideal was infrequently achieved except among wealthier families with adequate resources to support it.

Gainful employment for women was associated with lower caste status in India. Until recently, the denial of property rights to women further reduced their potential economic resources and their power. The custom of the purdah, which required the spatial segregation of women (men entered the women's quarters usually only for sexual purposes), prevented the more active participation of women in spheres outside of the home. The custom of purdah, incidentally, was introduced in northern India during the period of Muslim rule. It was not practiced in southern and western India.

The subordinate position of women in traditional India was ritualized in many other ways, most of them common in all extremely patriarchal societies. Deference patterns included the use of formal, respectful terms of address to the husband, who usually used familiar forms of address in response. Men ate first. They ate warmer food, and they ate the choicest morsels of food. Women and children ate what was left. Women stood when elder males entered the room and remained standing while in their presence.

Men and women (other than brothers and sisters) who were of the same generation did not sit together and talk. Husbands and wives did not joke with each other, since joking does not occur when extreme differences in authority exist between individuals. Women could talk freely to males of lower status— their young sons and nephews, for example. Among adults, however, gender was more important than age in determining deference and authority patterns. Sons, not widows, inherited the patriarch's property. Older women, therefore, deferred to younger adult males—their grown sons, for example.

Men and women did not engage in social or religious activities together. Women's recreational activities were home-centered, except for festivals or weddings; men's activities were community-centered. This pattern existed also in the play of young children. Even today, walking down the street in a rural village of almost any country with a strong patriarchal tradition, one sees little boys out playing. Little girls are nowhere in view.

Sex Roles in Arabic Countries. Arab countries in which the Muslim religion is practiced have also been characterized by extreme segregation of the sexes and surveillance of women, and by extreme subordination of women, at least formally (36). Conceptions of masculinity and femininity have differed somewhat from those of other patriarchal societies, however. The ideal male has been a fighter and a brave warrior, but he has been more expressive emotionally than has been typical of males in agricultural societies. Hard work and economic productivity, furthermore, have been defined as feminine traits in many Arab countries.

The "male vanity culture," in which males marketed and gossiped while women, particularly at low economic levels, farmed and produced handicrafts, provided at least a moderate degree of independence to lower status women. It is no accident that polygyny was more strongly institutionalized in Arabic cultures than in other agricultural societies, since this practice tends to occur where women have important economic provider roles. Nevertheless, the actual extent of polygyny appears to have been limited largely, although not entirely, to potentates with enormous material resources. Certainly the maintainance of a well-staffed harem was limited to the very wealthy—and the wealthy in agricultural societies are usually no more than 1 or 2 per cent of the population.

The great value placed on male erotic gratification in Arab cultures seems to have promoted a stronger emotional tie between husband and wife than is typical in patriarchal societies. Sexuality was defined as desirable and good in the Islamic religion, in Arabic literature, and in the folk heritage. The wife, according to the Koran, was highly valued as an object of erotic pleasure as well as a producer of male children. Women as well as men were viewed as very strongly endowed with sexual desire. This definition of female eroticism, combined with the emphasis on female chastity, promoted the practice of clitoridectomy and the seclusion of women in Arab societies.

The birthrate continues to be very high in Arab countries, even today, probably because of this stronger emphasis on sexuality. The traditional attitudes that Allah will provide, whatever the changing economic circumstances, and that fertility is an expression of the will of Allah, have lingered longer. These beliefs have been reinforced by a far less repressive attitude toward sex than is characteristic of Christian civilizations.

Although Muslim women in Arabic societies did much of the heavy, economically productive work, other factors also operated to enhance their status somewhat. Women were permitted to own some property in their own right. Dowries were usually converted by the bride's father into jewels and household goods that were given to the bride. These assets remained her own property, and she could sell them and retain the money. She was also freer to return home than women in traditional China, Japan, and India. Since most marriages took place between people from the same village or tribe, the bride was seldom obliged to sever relationships with her own family. Because she performed basic economic functions, and because the bride price was not returnable, her bargaining position was somewhat better, especially at the lower levels of society.

EMERGING MODERN VALUES. As societies develop technologically, and as scientific knowledge accumulates, certain values that are almost universal in traditional societies—familism, ethnocentrism, religiosity, fatalism, and authoritarianism—are gradually replaced by an opposite set of values. The modern values—individualism, tolerance and cosmopolitanism, secularism, rationalism, achievement and equalitarianism—become incorporated into the roles that men and women play, both in the family and in other spheres of life. These values affect sexual identity, and they transform typical expectations in the relationships between the sexes in modern societies.

The modern values are really urban values. They predate industrialization in that they existed to some extent in the large urban centers of preindustrial societies. I have called them modern values because they become much more prevalent in urbanized, industrial societies.

Individualism replaces familism as men and women seek formal education and employment in the nonfamily economy. The family loses its absolute control over its young and its adult women. As the standard of living rises, as opportunities grow, as mobility increases, individuals begin to place their own needs and wishes before those of their families. They begin to value self direction and independence above obedience and loyalty to family dictates and goals. Men will follow job opportunities even when this means breaking ties with relatives. Women will go out to work, even against opposition from other members of the family. The oldest child (male or female) will not willingly give up educational or other goals to support younger siblings or aged parents. Young people will choose marital partners (or cohabit without legal sanction) with or without the approval of their parents. The standard for the fulfilled life shifts from the discharge of family obligations to the fulfillment of individual needs—for both females and males.

Rationalism and secularism slowly replace religious standards in defining the relationship between men and women. Religion declines in influence in human societies as the realm of the uncertain, the mystifying, and the uncontrollable diminishes. Knowledge replaces faith as a guide to action and to human relationships. Priests take courses in psychology. Science undercuts dogma. When miracle drugs can save mothers' lives, death in childbirth is less likely to be viewed as God's will. When safe and effective techniques exist for contraception and abortion, women have more rational means for promoting their individual interests and desires. Religious doctrines are more likely to lose their hold when logical, dependable, and rational means are available for achieving secular goals.

As resources become more evenly distributed in modern societies, authoritarianism declines in the relationship between citizen and ruler, employer and employee, husband and wife, and parent and child. The middle class grows, and the masses become educated. Women go out to work increasingly and achieve more equal levels of education. Adult children may have more education and a higher income than their middle aged parents. Young children may potentially have more or fewer of these resources than their parents. Opportunity and the need for talent and drive in technologically developed societies play havoc with traditional conceptions of authority. Achievement and personality acquire greater significance; family, gender, birth order, and race become somewhat less important in determining identity, destiny, and power.

Ethnocentrism is the tendency to view the values and customs of one's own group as absolute and superior to others. It entails fear and hostility toward strangers and inability to understand or tolerate out-group differences. The opposite kind of orientation is involved in the idea of cultural relativism—in which one's own customs are seen as possibly arbitrary and certainly not the only good or required way to live.

People become less ethnocentric as they are brought up more permissively in more economically secure and more rapidly changing environments. They feel less aggression if they are less frustrated economically. If they are permitted to express aggression in the home more freely, they are less likely to displace their aggressive impulses onto out groups.

Ethnocentrism also declines as diverse peoples come into increasing contact with one another. This occurs directly as people move around more in technologically developed society, particularly as they move to urban centers. It occurs also as a result of education and exposure to the mass media. As ethnocentrism decreases, people become more sophisticated. They are less fearful of strange places and less suspicious of unfamiliar people. They are less rigid and more open to new and different ways of thinking and acting.

As individualism, rationalism, and educational and occupational opportunities increase, fatalism declines. Passive acceptance, as a way of life, is replaced by an active mastery orientation. More educated men and women, with more opportunity and more effective means at their disposal to achieve their goals, raise their expectations. They fight for what they want. Certain folk adages die out, such as: It is God's will; What will be, will be; It is written; That's life; Them's the breaks. New mottos appear, reflecting new circumstances: Nothing ventured, nothing gained; There's always room at the top; There'll be pie in the sky when you die; We shall overcome. Women with children return to school to complete their interrupted educations. Men change careers in middle age. Divorce rates rise in the later years of marriage. Little girls fight to get on all-male baseball teams. Little boys grow up to be social workers, nurses, and librarians. Sex typing breaks down as the belief in inevitability, predestination, and fate diminishes.

The modern values are emerging. They are far from universal, even in the most technologically advanced societies. Lower income groups in modern societies are more traditional, generally. They are less educated, and they are closer to their rural origins. Women tend to be more traditional than men. They are more familistic, more religious, more fatalistic, and more ethno centric. They tend to accept patriarchal attitudes, regardless of whether they abide by them. And when they do not, they usually feel guilt. Such women have not shared equally with men in access to higher education and to the most skilled occupations in modern societies. They have been more closely bound to the family—as children and as adults—and the family is the stronghold of tradition.

But all segments of modern societies—the races, the classes, the sexes, the generations, and the religious and ethnic groups —move toward the adoption of modern urban values. The rates vary according to the availability of educational and economic opportunities. Women in India are more apt to retain traditional values than women in the People's Republic of China, where the attempt to industrialize rapidly has been more successful.

The degree of adoption of modern values will also be related to the degree of isolation or exposure of the group to these values. Women living in ghettos, barrios, slums, and rural areas are less exposed than women who have been socially mobile. Housewives are less exposed than women who work. Also important here are the mass media, which provide models and techniques for achieving modern values and life styles.

Another major factor is the extent of discrimination experienced by various groups in their search for education and economic opportunity, and visibility is an important component of discrimination. Women and blacks are more visible than other segments of society. Religious discrimination (particularly when religion does not coincide with race) is usually less severe than discrimination based on race or gender. A Catholic or a Jew can occupy a position of leadership in American society more readily, usually, than a woman or a black. Black men earn less, on an average, than white men. White women earn less than black men. And black women have the lowest median incomes of any category of employees in the United States.

The strength of preexisting traditional values among various segments of the population, or in various societies, is another and final factor that affects the rate of adoption of the modern values. Where women have been very active in economic production in traditional societies, they will be more apt to move sooner into the partner role in modern societies. Middle class Jewish and black women in the contemporary United States are an example. They are much more likely to be gainfully employed than women of other races or religions. In areas of sub-Saharan Africa, southeast Asia, and the tribal regions of India, that have been characterized by "female farming systems," women are also better prepared to accept the new opportunities and the values that are promoted by industrialization (37). They may, however, experience an initial loss of status as the economy shifts away from agriculture and until there are adequate employment opportunities in the urban areas to which they migrate.

A review of the roles that men and women have played in major types of human societies, and of the changing values that become incorporated into these roles as societies develop technologically, points to a very important conclusion about sexual identity as this has varied historically. Women and men have not always regarded themselves as being very different in abilities and temperament, or as being very unequal in authority and in self worth. I have explained the historical differences in sex-typed identities and self evaluations of women and men largely in relation to developments in science and technology.

The same model can be applied to an understanding of present day variations in sexual identity in different parts of the world. These variations in identity are also related to technological development. But local values, stemming from unique historical circumstances, make for differences in the typical identities of men and women in various countries. These differences are not great—they are mainly a matter of degree; but they do illustrate the importance of somewhat different traditions in hindering or promoting change.

How do the roles and self images of men and women vary in contemporary societies around the world? To what extent have the modern values been incorporated into the typical expectations and orientations of men and women in various societies? In what ways have sexual identity, the status of women, and the degree of sex typing actually changed in societies that vary in level of technological development? And, finally, what have been the effects of political revolutions, preexisting ideologies, and new ideologies—socialism, for example—on the typical relationships between men and women in contemporary societies?

4 | Contemporary Variations: East and West

In an essay that attempts to bring together a great deal of information about varying sexual identities in human societies, it is impossible to cover the entire range of differences that exist and have existed. Thus my focus is on certain selected societies that reveal both the general trend as societies industrialize and certain unique variations that are a product of special historical circumstances in particular countries or geographic areas.

The effects of change on the self conceptions, emotions, and motivations of men and women in contemporary societies are not easy to convey simply by reciting facts about employment, education, sex typing, and sexual behavior. The battle between the old and the new has an internal dimension. This dimension is, perhaps, even more important than what is easily observable or measurable. For this reason, I include in my discussion first-person statements from autobiographies, diaries, and interviews of women and men whose identities and hopes are changing. This dramatically reveals the conflicts and the problems that people around the world are experiencing as they are exposed to new ideas, new values, new challenges, and new choices.

In all societies today, regardless of level of technological development, regardless of historical differences, and differences in past and present political and religious ideologies, the fact of being born male or female determines the core of the psychological identity of human beings. Despite major changes —in the roles of women, particularly—the traditional values are still quite prevalent even, again, in the most technologically advanced societies. Women, especially in the middle class, are far more apt to be employed in the nonfamily economy than in the past, but they are concentrated in lower level nonprofessional and nonadministrative jobs. They continue to work largely in sex-typed occupations—domestic service, clothing and canning industries, nursing, elementary school teaching, and social work —which are all related to women's traditional activities.

There has not been a fusing or sharing of roles, in which adults of both sexes are gainfully employed and share equal responsibility for homemaking and childrearing. Rather, all industrial societies have witnessed a gradual change in the obligations of women, who now perform what is called the "dual role." They have added outside employment, but they continue to be responsible for home and children.

The dual role for women is not new; it dates back to horticultural societies. In preindustrial societies, women who were poor also played the dual role in rural areas and in urban centers. It causes greater problems in industrial societies, however, because outside employment becomes more prevalent for all classes of women, and because the extended family is less likely to be available to help the mother with her homemaking and child care obligations.

Women have fewer children in modern societies, and many traditional homemaking chores are taken over by factories, laundries, cleaners, and restaurants; but standards of child care, sanitation, and comfort are raised. It is doubtful that modern women, if they play the dual role, have substantially more leisure than their predecessors. And, at least since the time of the invention of plant cultivation, women have probably had less leisure than men. Hunting, agriculture, and warfare have been periodic or seasonal activities. Industrial employment has been limited to specified hours—although these hours were very long in the early stages of industrialization. Homemaking and child-rearing, however, have not been limited by season, impulse, the time clock, or legislation.

The dual role is still typical even where official government policy has advocated the abolition of sex typing and the full equality of the sexes in rights, obligations, and status—in mainland China (1), the Soviet Union (2), and Sweden (3), for example. In these countries, too, women are largely excluded from the most skilled and the most powerful positions; typically, moreover, they tend to have lower self esteem than men.

Differences in the typical personality traits of the sexes also continue to exist in very different types of societies (4). Women around the world are more likely to be passive, conforming, and emotionally expressive. Men are more likely to be independent, achieving, and aggressive. These differences are diminishing, particularly among well-educated, urban populations in highly industrialized societies, but they persist in most contemporary societies.

Despite the rising status of women, the decline of arranged marriages, the growing belief in romantic love, greater premarital sexual freedom, the availability of safer and more effective contraceptives, and greater control over venereal disease, the double standard also persists, throughout the world.

SWEDEN. Sweden is a very progressive country in which enormous efforts have been made to equalize the status and identities of men and women. Premarital intercourse is almost universal, and about one-half of all Swedish brides are pregnant at marriage (as compared with approximately 20 per cent in the United States). In traditional Sweden, premarital pregnancy was valued as evidence of a young woman's childbearing capacities. It continues as a pattern that is not stigmatized in contemporary Sweden. But the double standard also continues in Sweden. A

majority of women have had only one or, at most, two partners
by the time they are married. A majority of males have had five
or more partners (5). Extramarital sex is strongly disapproved
for both sexes in Sweden, but occasional infidelity is more easily
forgiven in males than in females. And only about one-fourth of
the women in Swedish society report that sex is "wonderful"—
indicating, apparently, that a majority of Swedish women have
some problem about experiencing uninhibited sexual gratification, at least at times. This is true in America also, for most
women.

Sweden is an advanced welfare state. The government assumes almost total responsibility for the health, education, and
welfare of its citizens. Parents are granted family allowances for
each child. The aged receive full government pensions, regardless of need or previous contributions. Education is free at all
levels, as is medical care. Government-operated day care centers, where children may be placed in early infancy, are quite
numerous. Contraceptive devices and abortions are readily
available. Illegitimate children receive the same government allowance as legitimate children.

Government planning proceeds smoothly in Sweden, given a
small, homogeneous population, with fewer divergent values
and interests than are characteristic of societies such as the
United States. The absence of a national religion strongly emphasizing the traditional values is another factor that has promoted modernization in Sweden. The shortage of labor, and the
need to develop human resources in a country lacking many
natural resources, have promoted the greater utilization of the
talents of women in the nonfamily economy.

Girls attend machine shop courses in the elementary schools
in Sweden, and boys are taught cooking and sewing. The dual
role is still typical for women, however. The traditional values
have not disappeared in the relationship between the sexes, despite deliberate efforts to break down sex typing in the home
and on the job, and despite the opportunities and the advan-

tages of the welfare state, which tend to equalize the resources of men and women. The lag between changing objective conditions and persisting traditional values has not disappeared, although this lag is less extreme in Sweden than in most other countries. And the United States and Western Europe are moving in the direction of Sweden—more slowly, but very likely, inevitably.

CHINA. Mainland China also demonstrates the persistence of traditional values in the face of enormous government efforts to equalize the privileges of all citizens—young and old, male and female. The women's movement in the People's Republic of China is not viewed as a conflict between men and women, but in ideological terms, centering on the need to change the traditional values that linger, particularly among rural elements of the population (6).

The attempt to equalize the status and self esteem of women and men in China is symbolized by unisex clothing. Both sexes wear identical loose-fitting tunics and trousers. Women wear no cosmetics. The Cultural Revolution, which began in 1966, represented a massive attempt to wipe out traditional values—the "four olds": old ideas, old culture, old customs, and old habits (7). Before this time, it was not uncommon to see women dressed in traditional sheath dresses and wearing lipstick and rouge.

The family unit in China is nuclear, usually consisting of husband, wife, and from one to three children. Values have shifted in the direction of small families; children are no longer needed to till the fields, to worship ancestors (formal religion has all but disappeared), or as a source of support in old age. The aged are maintained by their local work units—factory or commune— and retire at 70 per cent of the pay they received while gainfully employed.

Most city families live in assigned one-room apartments. They are granted another room if aged parents live with them—a pattern that is not uncommon and is encouraged by the government. There are homes for the aged, but only a small proportion of those who are eligible live there (usually because they are disabled or because their children have been assigned jobs some distance away).

The new independence of women is indicated by the relative frequency of separation of husband and wife who work at jobs in different locations. The government attempts to place marital partners in jobs in the same city, but it is not always successful. Husbands and wives who are separated are granted periodic leaves to visit each other. Opposition to this pattern is apparently not strong, since it was not uncommon in traditional China.

The government frowns on premarital or extramarital sexual activity, equally for women and men, and the policy of discouraging such behavior appears to be successful (8). At the same time, late marriages (typically at age 26 for women and age 28 for men), are prescribed as one means of controlling the birthrate. Modern contraceptive techniques are readily available and widely used. Vasectomy is becoming increasingly popular.

Marriages are based on free choice and personal preference. There are no religious ceremonies; couples simply register their marriage at a municipal government office or farm commune center. Divorce is also relatively easy to obtain, although it is uncommon. If an attempt at reconciliation by a social worker in the factory or commune is unsuccessful, a couple is free to go to the local registry office and record the termination of their marriage.

Despite these revolutionary changes, traditional values survive. Male children are still preferred in China. Women have higher unemployment rates and are more likely to be fired when unemployment rises. They are underrepresented at the top occupational levels in industry, education, and government. They receive equal pay for the same work, but they are less likely to be employed in occupations requiring hard manual labor, which are more highly paid in China than lighter manual work.

Role segregation in the home has declined, especially among the younger generations. Women continue to play the dual role, however, even though day care centers are more available in China than in other socialist countries. The problem of securing the services of stable, loving mother substitutes in day care centers, incidentally, does not appear to exist in China. "Aunties," as nursery teachers are called, rarely leave their assigned jobs. Moreover, they share the values, goals, and educational philosophies of the parents—a situation that does not obtain in countries like the United States, where values and interests are far more diverse.

The rising status of women in mainland China, as symbolized by freer communication between the sexes and personal preference as a basis for marriage, is more accepted by the young than the old. In the following account, a thirty-two-year-old, literate woman, living in the provinces and working to organize and train women to understand and use modern skills and techniques, describes the survival of traditional attitudes and identities in her village—particularly among older citizens:

> . . . there are no great problems. One gets those mostly with the older people. That goes for marriage: some of the older people do not believe in marriage of free will. "How can a girl run off with the first chap she sees?" the older women ask. We have to talk to them and make propaganda for the new marriage. We have to remind them of how they felt when they were young and how they were made to suffer under the old system of marriage. It isn't so often it ever comes to a real conflict, but we did have a case in 1960.
>
> That was when Tuan Fu-yin's eighteen-year-old daughter, Tuan Ai-chen, fell in love with a boy from Seven-mile Village. But her parents refused to let her marry. They said that the boy was poor and that they wanted to marry her to somebody better off. One evening Tuan Ai-chen

came to me and wept and complained. I went with her to her cave and talked with her parents. I said to them: "You have no right to prevent your daughter from marrying, you know that, don't you? Purchase marriage is not allowed in the new society. It is a crime to sell your daughter these days. Before, you could sell your daughter like a cow, but you can't do that any longer." I told them about the things that used to happen in the old days, about girls drowning themselves in wells, of girls hanging themselves and that sort of thing, about all the unhappiness purchase marriage caused. At first, Tuan Fu-yin tried to stand up to me. He said: "I had to pay dearly for my wife. Now I have been giving this girl food and clothes. I have brought her up and she just goes off. It isn't right. I just lose and lose all the time. I must get back something of all the money I have laid out on her. If she can't fall in love with a man who can pay back what she's cost, then it isn't right for her to marry."

I talked a long time with them that evening, and in the end I said: "You don't live badly in the new society. If you ever have difficulties, your daughter and son-in-law will help you. They are not rich, but they won't refuse to help you." Then they replied: "We must think about it." The next time I went there, only the girl's mother was at home. She had thought about it and she now told me her own story. I hadn't known it, otherwise I would have made use of it on the first occasion. She said: "I was sold to Tuan Fu-yin when I was a little girl. I was sold in the same way you sell a goat. But my parents got a lot for me. Tuan's father had to take out a loan. That made them nasty to me. I was forced to work hard so as to make the loan worth while. They were all nagging at me. I can remember how much I used to cry. Now that I think of that, I don't want my daughter to marry someone she can't like." Then she wept. Tuan Fu-yin didn't say anything more. But such cases are rare. It is the only one I remember. Tuan Fu-yin's own sons had been allowed to marry in the new way, of course, because that meant that he did not need to pay anything for his daughters-in-law.

Another thing we have to deal with now and again is that the old women find it difficult to understand that nowadays women laugh and joke with men. They scold their daughters and daughters-in-law and granddaughters for not observing decent behaviour. When that happens, we have to speak with the old women about the equality of the sexes. We tell them that, now, a woman is the equal of a man in the family and in society. She does not just look after the home, she also works in the fields. She has to vote and she can be elected. It is obvious that she also talks with men and jokes with them as comrades. We remind the old people about their own bitter youth and keep telling them that as women now are equal, they also have the right to chat and joke. The old people say that they agree we are right. But in their heart of hearts they always feel uneasy and uncertain when they see girls joking with men. But we are patient with the old people. They can't help their attitude. Perhaps not all old women are like that, but most, I'm sure, think it indecent and immoral and shocking that young people talk with each other. The young people, of course, are all agreed. None of the young people think like the old ones on this question. So it will solve itself in time.

From *Report From A Chinese Village* by Jan Myrdal. Translated by Maurice Michael. Copyright © 1965 by William Heinemann Ltd. Reprinted by permission of Pantheon Books, a division of Random House Inc., pp. 224–226.

JAPAN. Although the traditional values have not entirely disappeared in the relationships between the sexes in China, the changes that have occurred are remarkable in view of the strength of preexisting patriarchal values. Japan, on the other hand, despite a far more developed technology and all the concomitant changes, clings more to traditional sex role conceptions. We see here the importance of ideology in facilitating or hindering value changes. Earlier and more rapid industrialization notwithstanding, Japan lags behind China in equalizing the status and privileges of men and women. Government policy

has not been directed toward effecting this change, and it has
not occurred to the extent that it has in China (9). Even within
the urban middle classes, most women in Japan continue to
have very low self esteem, relative to men.

Women attend the universities in Japan, but an informal
quota exists. The percentage of women in the professions is low,
despite a tradition of nonfamily gainful employment of women
in the entertainment field (from geishas to prostitutes) and the
important productive roles of women in the countryside. On the
other hand, the role of wife and mother appears to have more
prestige in Japan than it has in the United States. This factor
may limit the push of women into the industrial economy.

Rationalism is highly valued by Japanese women, however.
The mass media have depicted Western techniques for more ef-
ficient housekeeping, and Japanese technology has provided laborsaving devices that are enthusiastically purchased and used.
The traditionally elaborate and time-consuming methods of food
preparation are fast disappearing.

Abortion and the use of contraception are widespread, particularly in the cities, although the practice of female infanticide
appears to continue in the countryside. Many more male than
female infants survive the first year of life, a reversal of the
usual pattern in societies where infants are cared for equally
well, regardless of sex.

The nuclear family is becoming typical, particularly in the cities. The burden of the two dependent generations—the young
and the old—is more severe for the nuclear family in Japan
than in other countries where such government welfare measures as social security are available.

Formal rituals—forms of address, for example—continue to
symbolize status differences between the generations and the
sexes. In leisure activities, particularly, separation of husband
and wife persists, although this custom is changing somewhat in
the large cities. Women are expected to exercise more control
over erotic and aggressive impulses than men, although self-con-

trol continues to be an ideal for both sexes.

In an intensely competitive and perfectionist society, the tendency for women to achieve vicariously through their sons is reinforced, if the opportunity and the desire for women to achieve outside the family sphere is absent or minimal. The binding mother–son relationship remains strong in Japan, at the expense of female self realization, male independence, and a closer husband–wife tie. The traditional practice of sleeping with children, all together, or parent and child separately, continues in the countryside. This is another indication of the greater value placed on the parent–child rather than the husband–wife relationship.

Companionship in marriage is an ideal that is promoted in the mass media, but the continued presence of large numbers of hostesses and bar girls in present-day Japan indicates that husband and wife still tend to be separated in social life. The double standard is still quite strong. Stronger negative sanctions are attached to infidelity on the part of the wife, even in revenge for a husband's adultery, than on male infidelity.

Probably companionship and free and intimate communication will not become an important characteristic of the relationship between husband and wife in Japan until the practice of arranged marriage, which is still prevalent, dies out (10). Expectations differ in marriages based on arrangement than in those based on personal preference and romantic love. Wives in arranged marriages tend to expect little more of the husband than the capacity to play out his role as economic provider successfully. Men expect that their physical and erotic needs will be taken care of and that children—male heirs, particularly— will be born.

The persistence of arranged marriages in Japan, despite the increasing economic independence of adult children and the declining influence of the extended family, is probably due at least in part to the continuing segregation of the sexes at school, at work, and in recreational activities. Under these conditions, it is

extremely difficult to engage in informal trial and error heterosexual relationships in which mutual liking and understanding
can build up. A similar situation exists in contemporary India,
where the sexes are highly segregated, as in the past.

Where overpopulation is a problem, women are less likely to
be employed in the industrial economy. If welfare state reforms
are minimal, there will be fewer jobs in the health, education,
and welfare fields—where women tend to be concentrated in
more highly industrialized societies. When opportunities are
limited, women everywhere are the last to be hired and the first
to be fired. Marital partners in modern societies are usually
found in places of work or study. Thus the practice of arranged
marriage is likely to continue if women are largely excluded
from educational and occupational opportunities, because of
overpopulation and a lack of jobs other than in domestic service
or segregated factory work.

Two excerpts from recent portraits of Japanese women illustrate the persistence of arranged marriage, the continued psychological separation of husband and wife, the extreme
differences in the status and self esteem of the sexes, and the en-
during emphasis on conformity and obedience in modern Japan.
The women described are urban, educated, upper middle class
women—a group that has usually been in the forefront of
change in modernizing and modern countries:

> Wondering where my sister could be, I knelt down beside
> her writing desk. Everything was in its place as usual—a
> shining letterbox inlaid with gold, with crimson tassels of
> silk, a calligraphy set in varnished brown, a small ivory
> statue of the Virgin Mary, and a string of crystal beads
> that belonged to my grandmother.
>
> Beside the bamboo brush stand something square and
> flat, neatly folded in white paper caught my eye. I took it
> up, hesitated, then without opening the wrapping placed
> it on the desk exactly as it lay before I touched it. I knew
> what it was—a photograph of the bridegroom, my older
> sister's future husband. Suddenly, I felt as if I were doing

something wrong being in her room, alone, while she was away. The quietness of the room, and the little white statue made me feel like a stranger.

Perhaps I shouldn't ask her anything, I thought, slowly climbing the polished wooden stairs to my nursery.

Weeks passed, but there was no change in my sister's demeanor. As usual she played the thirteen-stringed lyre, arranged flowers, embroidered cherry blossoms on a black satin cloth, and read her favorite poems from the classics. Then finally the day of the formal meeting came.

She looked beautiful that morning—in a deep lilac kimono with white peonies blossoming out on the hem, her long, shiny black hair drawn back in a neat little bun, coral brooch on a brocade sash, and a touch of powder on her slight oval face.

"*Itte mairimasu*—I shall go but to return," she said, tipping her head a little to the side, as she always did when speaking to people.

"If you don't like the way he looks, say so frankly," said Father. "No use being bashful about such things."

My sister blushed, and turned away.

That evening Mother looked thoughtful. "It's an important decision, Mariko San," she said. "So think well over it. If you don't want to go, it is not too late to refuse. . ."

"I—don't know, Mother," my sister replied hesitantly. "I hoped—to stay home a little longer. Perhaps. . ."

"But remember, Mariko San," interrupted Mother, "a woman has to get married sooner or later, for that is her duty. You might be happy, and then again you might not be. But in life. . ." Mother stopped, as if searching for words. Then she added, a little sadly, "In life—a woman cannot expect too much happiness. So think it over carefully, Mariko San."

"I would rather leave it to you and Father," my sister answered in a low voice. "I would rather not decide by myself. . ."

From *Rain And The Feast Of The Stars* by Reiko Hatsumi, pp. 23–24. Reprinted by permission of Houghton Mifflin Co. © 1959 by Reiko Hatsumi Allen.

Her brother always got the biggest helpings at meals. If they had fish, he got the largest one. This irritated Kazuko.

"Why does he have so much nicer fish?" she once asked.

"Because he is the first son," said her mother.

"But why does he have better fish as the first son?" she persisted.

"Because he is going to inherit the family estate."

In fact, he got everything he wanted. The rest deferred to him and served him. All this he took for granted. He had the largest and best room to himself. The three daughters shared a much smaller one at the back of the house. This was because the daughters were expected to marry soon and leave the family. They were considered temporary. She learned later that this was liberal and represented progress as compared with earlier generations of their family. In those days large helpings of fish or meat were served to the father and eldest son. If that exhausted the supply, the other went without.

Kazuko's father, although not particularly progressive, was rather generous and easygoing, so the traditional strictness was imperceptibly relaxed, but in other families she observed many strange things, the matter of baths, for example.

Bathing in Japan is not a mere utilitarian matter of hygiene or cleanliness but also of comfort, relaxation, and even of aesthetic enjoyment and sociability. The bath is a big wooden tub of very hot water with a charcoal heater built in—or in a bathhouse or hotel, it is a tank. The actual washing is done outside the tub. The bather gets in, submerges to the neck, and stays. The same hot water is used by all the members of the family in succession—all scrubbing themselves first.

There is a regular order for bathing—father, sons, in order of age, mother, daughters, servants. While this was still true in Kazuko's house, the order could on occasion be changed for convenience.

When Kazuko was ten her mother went to visit a cousin and took her along. They arrived in the late eve-

ning after a tiresome trip and their hostess considerately
prescribed an early bath and early to bed. After they
were through they heard her call her oldest son, about
Kazuko's age, to come and take his bath. Then they heard
her call him a second and third time. Finally she went to
his room.

"Your sisters and I, and the servants are all of us wait-
ing our turn," she said. "Take your bath soon."

"I do not care to bathe tonight," he said, "when two
women have taken their baths ahead of me."

Reprinted with the permission of Farrar, Straus and Gi-
roux, Inc. from *Daughters of Changing Japan* by Earl
Herbert Cressy, pp. 31–33. Copyright © 1955 by Earl
Herbert Cressy.

"You are not going out again tonight, are you?" Kazuko burst out. "And with that man?"

He looked at her half-drunkenly.

"Come and wish me a happy evening," he ordered
with maudlin courtesy.

Without a word she came and bowed him out formally
at the door, repeating the required polite formula.

For a long time she remained thus, on her hands and
knees, her forehead almost to the matting. She heard their
voices die away down the street. She followed their steps
in her imagination. She pictured the girls in the geisha
house pouring sake for them.

This was the end. She had become one of the "unfor-
tunate housewives," like the wife of the barber near
their old home in Tokyo. There was no use thinking of
leaving. She had no place to go. A divorce, if she could
manage it, would merely lead to year after year of office
drudgery by day and a lonely room at night. There was
only one thing to be done.

Next morning she put her house in order. She walked
to the shore of a little lake just outside the city. She filled
the long sleeves of her kimono with stones. She found a
place where the bank of the lake was high enough. She
stood on the edge and looked down at the peaceful water.

One convulsive moment and it would be over. She gathered herself for the plunge.

Suddenly a rush of thoughts and images flooded through her mind. She saw herself falling. She saw herself drowned. She thought wildly of the twins. Who would care for them? She pictured her empty home. Who would look after it? But of course the solution was simple. He would marry again. All this was a situation that could not be escaped. It had to be endured. If she dropped out, another woman would be brought in and would have to bear it. But they were *her* children. It was her home. After all, he was her husband. These were her responsibilities.

She started taking the stones out of her sleeves, and when one rolled down and splashed into the lake she shuddered.

She told Yoko she had really died at that time.

What remained was the stereotype of an individual, stamped out by the relentless pressure of Japanese society —the conventional, obedient wife, serving her husband; the fond mother of her children, meticulous in every detail of their welfare; the good neighbor, observant of the local folkways, saying and doing the right thing at the right time, smiling with just the right degree of cordiality; selfless.

Reprinted with the permission of Farrar, Straus and Giroux, Inc. from *Daughters of Changing Japan* by Earl Herbert Cressy, pp. 304–305. Copyright © 1955 by Earl Herbert Cressy.

THE SOVIET UNION. As in China and Japan, the relationship between the sexes in today's Soviet Union indicates the effects of special and unique historical conditions in addition to technological and ideological factors. Technologically, the Soviet Union is almost as advanced as Japan and far ahead of China. Ideologically, Marxist principles underlie government policy with respect to the status and role of the sexes in China

and in the Soviet Union. But the enormous loss of manpower experienced in the Soviet Union during World War I resulted in a
large surplus of women and a population decline. The Revolution, the Civil War, famines, epidemics, purges and World War
II added their toll, through the years. The resulting labor shortage modified the application of Marxist principles to the relationship between men and women in the Soviet Union in very
significant ways. On the one hand, the population shortage led to
encouraging the gainful employment of women. At the same
time, however, it required an emphasis on childbearing, which,
in the absence of adequate child care provisions, is inconsistent
with the demands of gainful employment of women (11).

Following the Russian Revolution; much legislation was
aimed at promoting equality between the sexes and raising the
status of women. Marriage and divorce procedures were simpli-
fied. Abortion was legalized. Illegitimacy was not stigmatized,
morally or legally. The family was expected to wither away as
an economic and childrearing unit, its functions reduced solely
to reproduction and the provision of psychological gratification
for family members. Large numbers of women were recruited
into public industry. They took the heavier, less skilled jobs
usually because women were less educated and because the goal
then, and until very recently, was to develop heavy industry
first, and as rapidly as possible.

Women who did not work were defined as parasites, living off
the body politic without contributing adequately to its growth.
Family life and economic life were to be communalized and col-
lectivized. Yet in conflict with these goals was the survival of
traditional patriarchal attitudes, and perhaps even more important, the necessity to promote childbearing, to replace the deci-
mated population. By 1936, as labor shortages persisted, divorce
regulations became more stringent, and abortions could no
longer be obtained legally. Heroine mothers—producers of large
numbers of potential workers—received special economic rewards and honors. Child care facilities were expanded some-

what, particularly in industries that employed women. Parents of small families were taxed, as were unmarried individuals of childbearing age. The policy toward illegitimacy, before and since then, vacillated according to the need of Soviet society for workers.

Traditional values, less collectivistic than in China, hindered the commune movement. The emphasis on heavy industry diverted resources necessary to provide universal child care facilities, communal kitchens, adequate housing, and other consumer services. Soviet women are more apt to be employed in the industrial economy than any other female workers (with the possible exception of those in present-day China). Thus now, as in the past, they suffer from the conflicts and stresses of the dual role to a greater extent than women anywhere else in the world.

The early days of industrialization were even harder on women than on men. Although the life expectancy of both sexes has doubled since the Revolution, the gap between male and female life expectancy was very low until recently (12). In the 1960s, it was eight years (the average life expectancy of females was seventy-five; for males it was sixty-seven) This approaches the figures for other highly industrialized nations and indicates that the pressures on Soviet women are easing.

In the Soviet Union, women who play the dual role have far less leisure time than men. Husbands and sons do not typically help in the home. The babushkas—grandmothers, who were widowed in a large numbers during World War II—frequently helped working mothers with child care tasks in the past. But now the babushkas are dying off, or they are themselves employed or going to school. The problem of establishing adequate child care facilities and providing other services to lighten the burden of the employed wife and mother persists. There is little domestic help available in the Soviet Union, few laborsaving devices, and few conveniences such as supermarkets and prepackaged foods.

Despite the ideology of equality, women workers continue to

be concentrated largely in semiskilled and unskilled manual labor, rather than in white collar occupations, as in the United States. In government, industry, and education, and within the Communist party, women are increasingly underrepresented as one proceeds up the scale of higher professional and administrative levels. Yet women are in a majority in professions such as medicine. Very likely this is because of the previous shortage of male workers and because medicine, like nursing, requires nurturing qualities that have been traditionally sex typed as feminine. Nevertheless, even in the medical profession, women are usually employed in clinical capacities rather than in the more prestigious teaching and research jobs.

Soviet women, however, have made more gains in the educational and occupational spheres than women in any other country—again with the possible exception of China. (We have no figures for China.) Now that the more pressing need to develop heavy industry is abating, government policy is directed increasingly toward developing consumer industries and services. At the moment, this goal is not being reached. Heavy industry continues to develop, but light industries and consumer services are suffering all kinds of setbacks. Eventually, the strain of the dual role for women will be eased considerably, but the direction of change may not proceed in the way that the Soviet government has anticipated.

In 1956 Khrushchev announced plans to build a network of boarding schools that would eventually house all infants and children in the Soviet Union. A beginning was made, but plans were later changed because of negative popular reaction. Most parents objected to a total separation from their children. The less educated and less well-paid segments of the population were more apt to use these facilities than higher income groups.

The advantages of boarding schools were and are more apparent to parents who live under crowded housing conditions, who are more pressed by high food prices, and who feel that the more educational benefits their children have, the better their

start will be in life. Public child care institutions in the Soviet
Union offer a good diet, as well as early and systematic training
in the development of maturational skills and skills in music,
language, dance, and academic subjects.

More highly educated people are less pressed by economic
circumstances to turn over their children entirely to other agen-
cies. They are more confident than poorer parents of their ability
to provide an adequate intellectual environment for their offspring. This was indicated in a recent survey of 2,000 women
workers in the Moscow area (13). More skilled women who
were engaged in more "creative" work were less likely to use
day care facilities than unskilled working mothers.

Not only did the more highly educated women spend more
time with their children, they reported greater satisfaction with
their role as mothers. In the United States, also, working mothers, particularly in the middle class, report greater satisfactions
with motherhood than those who stay at home full-time (14).
The more highly educated women workers in the Soviet Union
also spend much less time on routine household chores, and this
discrepancy cannot have to do entirely with income differences,
since consumer services that are available are cheap. More
highly educated women are more apt to have internalized the
modern values. They are more rational in their approach to
homemaking. In addition, they are more apt to find psychological gratification in their relationships with their (fewer, planned
and wanted, and less economically burdensome) children.

For these reasons, the boarding school movement has declined in the Soviet Union. Instead, there has been an increase
in the number of "schools of the prolonged day," which are day
care centers that operate until 6 P.M., infants and children re-
turning home for the night. Even these institutions are very limited in number, however. According to one source, only about
10 per cent of all Soviet infants under two years of age are enrolled in public nurseries; 20 per cent of the children between
the ages of three and six are in preschool institutions, and

boarding schools enroll about 5 per cent of the children who are seven years old or older (15). However, almost all these infants and children come from the lower educational and occupational groups.

The dual role remains a source of strain for Soviet women. As Soviet society continues to industrialize, however, as educational levels rise and as unskilled and semiskilled jobs are increasingly automated out of existence, we can anticipate certain changes in the roles of men and women. These changes will probably become universal in computerized and automated societies. (And they will probably occur first in the United States.)

Very likely, day care centers will become far more widespread in the Soviet Union (and elsewhere) than they are at present. They will not be "prolonged care" centers or boarding schools, however. The work week will be gradually shortened. Part-time employment, for women first, then probably for men also, will become typical. Employed parents will have more time to spend with their children, and day care centers will operate on a shorter day.

The trend toward more part-time employment is just beginning in the United States. Employers are discovering that it is sometimes more profitable to employ two part-time workers than one full-time worker—particularly in jobs that are not extremely complicated. Part-time workers are less tired during their shorter working hours. They work more efficiently, they have lower absentee rates, and they are less likely to engage in time stretchers such as coffee breaks. Eventually, as productivity and national wealth increase (and if too great a percentage of this wealth is not preempted by the upper classes), what is now defined as part-time employment will merge with what will then be the average work week for all employees. Income from these two types of employment situations will also become increasingly equal.

These trends will promote greater sharing of work and homemaking and childrearing obligations by men and women. We are now experiencing a lag in this respect in all countries. Women are more willing to work outside the home, but men are not equally willing to share in homemaking and childrearing chores, particularly when the wife does not work because of economic necessity (16).

Traditional values are resistant, but they cannot ultimately override the effects of the objective changes in life circumstances that are brought about by technological and scientific developments. As values continue to change in the direction of increasing equalitarianism, as women become more independent and more insistent on mutuality in all spheres of life, we can anticipate a greater decline in the segregation of the sexes, at home, at work, and at play—in all societies.

Economists have estimated that if trends since the turn of the twentieth century continue, the average work week in the United States in the year 2000 will be approximately fifteen hours. This is a consequence of constantly increasing levels of productivity. According to conservative estimates, the actual purchasing power of the average family in the United States will at least double, and very likely triple, by the year 2000. The Soviet Union and other highly industrialized nations can be expected to follow the same pattern. The number of jobs available will decline because of automation, but employment opportunities will very likely be spread out among more people—including women. More women will work in the nonfamily economy, and not for economic reasons alone.

The identity of women will change. It will more often include self conceptions as independent, assertive, competent human beings—qualities that are associated with gainful employment and higher levels of education. Males, too, will change. Historically, when men have had less authority in relation to their wives and children e.g., in matrilineal societies and in industrial societies after retirement), they have related more warmly to their families. In modern societies, the retired grandfather is an expressive, rather than an authority figure. More males, there-

fore, can be expected to display expressive and nurturing qualities, which reflect declining patriarchalism. Such personality
traits will better equip men to fulfill the husband and father
roles as currently defined. Expectations in modern families shift
toward psychological support, companionship, mutual identification, and friendship among all members of the family, including husband and father.

In America, at least some members of the women's movement
have begun to expand their goals beyond the equalizing of the
political and economic rights of women. They speak and write
of the necessity to realize *human* potential—female and male.
They deplore the destructive effects of excessive competition
and compulsive striving for material success on both sexes.

The average life expectancy for males is lower in the United
States than it is in a number of other highly industrialized nations. The gap between the life expectancies of males and females (about nine years) is higher. Citizens of the wealthiest
nation in the world do not have the longest life expectancy
because the American government has failed to solve the problem of poverty—particularly among blacks. Life expectancy
figures are averages, taking into account infant mortality rates,
among other variables. And the United States has higher infant
mortality rates than a number of more reform-oriented modern
nations.

The larger gap between male and female life expectancies in
America reflects the higher male infant mortality rate. (Male infants, remember, are more susceptible to the stresses of physical
deprivation than female infants.) Also, however, it reflects the
effects of excessive striving, of moonlighting, and of unbounded
materialism on adult males in the United States. The toll has
been more severe for men than for women in American society,
at least up to now.

Each country, as it industrializes, accumulates its own unique
history. In the long run (and in many cases, the long, long run),
all seem to change along similar lines, however, with respect to

the identities, status, and behavior of its male and female citizens.

European countries generally experienced large losses of manpower during World War II, although not so large as did the Soviet Union. Losses in the United States were comparatively minimal. Therefore, the postwar baby boom was most pronounced in the United States, whereas the postwar shortage of labor in many European countries promoted the continued employment and recruitment of women into all occupations, including those sex-typed for men.

In the early 1970s despite differences in national traditions, many European countries have a larger percentage of women employed at the higher occupational levels than does the United States. For example, 7 per cent of American doctors are women, but the figure for West Germany is 20 per cent; for Denmark, 16.4 per cent, for Sweden, 15.4 per cent, and for the Soviet Union, 75 per cent (17). The percentage of women doctors in America in 1970 was lower than in pre-Castro Cuba (18).

This illustrates an important point about the role of women in industrializing countries, incidentally. Because of the shortage of skilled personnel of either sex, women from the upper, more highly educated classes in some developing countries have found it easier to break into more prestigious occupations that are essential to the well-being of the society. They are less apt to be viewed as competitive and unfeminine, and the individuals themselves are less conflicted about their achievement drives, since these are defined in terms of patriotic duty rather than the pursuit of self interest. The women's movement in countries outside the United States is not directed against men, as it tends to be in America. The target is the economic system that exploits both sexes, or the traditional values that women are even more likely to retain than men.

The role of women in industrializing countries varies, however, depending in part on the size of the population—particularly the size of the middle class population. If enough

118 CONTEMPORARY VARIATIONS: EAST AND WEST

middle class sons are being produced, or if too many are available, for the number of professional and administrative jobs in the economy, women are more apt to be kept out of higher level jobs. Government policy in creating and subsidizing higher level occupations, especially in the health, education, and welfare fields, is also crucial in this respect. In India, for example, there is a tremendous shortage of teachers and other professionals in rural areas. But training facilities and salaries for teachers are abysmally inadequate. Thus the potential pool of talent in the teaching field remains largely untapped. In recruiting women professionals to work in rural areas in India, the surviving traditional attitudes of seclusion of women pose another problem, for in such societies, women are less likely to leave the protection of their families to work alone in a strange community.

The pattern of seclusion of women can promote opportunities for women, however. If only women are permitted to work with women patients or clientele, the job market for women is expanded. In India, again, there is a glut of educated women relative to the supply of white collar jobs, but there is a shortage of workers in the sex-segregated health professions—nursing, midwifery, and related occupations (19).

Another factor affecting employment opportunities for both men and women is the unwillingness of city born and reared professionals, managers, and government officials to live and work in isolated, provincial rural areas. In most countries, including the United States, when professionals, administrators, and others have had a choice about where they work, they have preferred the cities. The Soviet Union and China, with their planned economies, have attempted to solve the problem by assigning people to jobs in rural areas, according to local need. This policy has expanded gainful employment opportunities for women. The jobs are there potentially—in terms of the needs of the population.

All urbanized, industrialized societies must try to provide adequate funds to pay workers in the health, education, and wel-

fare fields, and they must see that the workers are spread out
proportionately in all geographic areas. In nonsocialist countries, the problem may be solved eventually on a voluntary
basis, as reform orientations become more widespread and as
communication and transportation facilities continue to improve, thus diminishing the isolation of rural areas.

Soviet women have had a head start on other women in that
the equalization of the status of the sexes has been an aspect of
official government policy for two generations. That they are not
clearly in the vanguard of the economic, political, and psychological liberation of women around the world, at the moment, is
probably due largely to the economic problems that the Soviet
Union has experienced in trying to industrialize rapidly. The
deemphasis on consumer services has delayed the progress of
women, but so has the survival of patriarchal attitudes in Soviet
society.

To illustrate the emergence of the "new woman" in the Soviet
Union, after the Revolution, I have chosen an excerpt from the
diary of a young Russian woman, begun at the age of fifteen, in
1936. The author was killed at the front during World War II.

Nina Kosterina, the daughter of a middle class journalist and
Communist party member, reveals in this short passage an
achievement orientation that is strongly encouraged and rewarded by her father. She has been drawn out into political activities, as well, through her membership in the Komsomol, the
youth organization of the Communist party. Her diary, a deeply
personal document, nevertheless contains numerous references
to political events and news about nationally known figures. It
reveals the enthusiasms, the expanding consciousness, and the
self confidence and self pride of a modern woman.

June 20

Exams are over, I am an eighth-year student! And suddenly, out of nowhere, came the feeling—I shall keep a
diary. Said, and done. But what shall I call it? I thought

about it for a long time. I began to ask myself: Who am
I? What am I? I have no talents of any kind. . . . And,
thinking of how untalented I am, I decided to call my
diary "The Diary of an Ordinary Girl." Completely ordinary. I don't even dream of anything special. Other girls
dream of becoming doctors, engineers. To me, the future
is utterly hidden, in a fog.

I want to begin my diary with a date that is most vivid in
my memory. It was April 8th, my fifteenth birthday. I
gave a party, and my guests were Alik, Boris, Volodya,
Volya, Lusya, Tonya, and Vitya. Before the party, I was
terribly nervous, afraid that everybody would be bored.
But the evening went beautifully—I've never had so
much fun at a birthday party. Also, this was the first time
that I "ventured" to dance with boys—with Alik and
Vitya. When Alik put his arm around my waist, and I put
my hand on his shoulder, a shiver ran through me—it was
such an exciting and happy feeling, I have been dancing
for a long time, I love to dance, but I have never enjoyed
it so much before. Alik was fooling around and lifted me
up in the air. My heart stopped, I could not catch my
breath, and my cheeks flamed. . . .

Afterward we played forfeit games, and Alik and I kissed.
The first time, he kissed me; the second time, I kissed
him, when he was saying good-bye. We also played "flirt
of the flowers." Volodya and Lusya turned it into a flirta-
tion between themselves. I did not like the game and
stopped playing. There were other games too. Everybody
stayed late, until eleven o'clock.

It was a good party. It reinforced my friendship with the
boys, but cooled off my relations with the girls. Ogloblina
was especially angry and later called me a "toady." There
were many arguments about that, and finally she was
transferred to another class.

The May Day celebrations were very gay. We marched
in demonstrations across the Red Square; I saw all the
leaders. We sang, danced, shouted. . . . And in the evening we went to see the operetta *The Bird Seller*. I loved
it.

I must also tell about the visit to the Museum of Fine
Arts. I went with the whole family. But in the museum I

went off my myself: I wanted to see whatever I felt like, and to look at it as long as I felt like. There were many things I liked, but best of all was a certain French painting: a seacoast, ships in the distance, beautiful, branching trees on the shore, and a crowd of people stretching their arms toward the sea in panic and despair. There was also an English painting—a woman in a gray dress, with a riding crop in her hand, standing on a veranda.

But the conclusion I drew from this visit to the museum was that I must go again, and next time with a guide.

Now I must make a record for myself of the important events of this period: Gorky died, and a draft for a new Constitution has been published. The Constitution is something I understand very little, although I feel that this is an event of great importance to our country. But Gorky's death was like a personal sorrow to me. We have his complete works. I've read many of them, and some stirred me so much that I could not sleep. And now, Gorky is gone. . . .

There was also a lot of anxiety in connection with my admission to the Komsomol. I have, generally, been reading the newspapers, but all the same I had to go to father for help. He talked to me for two hours, reminding me about many things and explaining others, especially about the Constitution. After the talk with him, I went to the District Committee of the Komsomol quite calmly. What a father I have! There were ten of us at the District Committee, and everybody was nervous. I did not like the District Committee office: dirty, with smudged, dingy walls, nowhere to sit down. It seemed to me that I was calm, but others said that I came out of the office white as chalk. They gave me a membership card, tiny-tiny, white.

At home I showed it to papa. He caught me in his arms and threw me up and kissed me. "Good girl, Ninok!" He said it in such a way that I was filled with joy and pride.

Oh, yes, I almost forgot about something that applies to us women: publication of a draft law to forbid abortions. One evening, I read reports by three Polish women about life in Poland, where women give birth to their babies right by the machines they operate, in the marketplace, in

ditches. . . . I was so upset that when I went to bed I
buried my nose in the pillow and burst out crying.

Let me list the books I have read lately. I read Kochin's
Peasant Girls. I liked it very much. Hugo's *The Man Who
Laughs* almost made me flunk the physics test—I got so
absorbed in reading, I forgot that I had to prepare for the
exam.

During examination days I went twice to Kamerny The-
atre and saw the movie *The Circus* three times. Orlova is
marvelous!

During exams, papa made a promise: if I did well, we
would go to Khvalynsk. Yesterday was the last exam—
geography. I passed. I've graduated from the Seven-Year
School. Hurrah, we are going to Khvalynsk!

Taken from *THE DIARY OF NINA KOSTERINA*, translated by Mirra Ginsburg, pp. 13–16. © 1968 by Mirra
Ginsburg. Used by permission of Crown Publishers, Inc.

The following excerpts from Russian newspaper accounts of
two young marriages reveal the strain of the dual role in a student marriage (which later ended in divorce), and the shift from
the traditional to the modern in a working class marriage.

We talked about the institute. The whole room—the table,
the window sill, the chairs—was covered with open
books, but you could feel that Tanya was not touching
them. She tried to study in the evening when the baby
slept, yet she didn't make any progress and the year was
wasted. Tanya was alone for days at a time. Volodya had
some kind of important community work, and at night he
had to earn money, so he came home very late—sleepy,
tired, and irritable.

And I heard the words that have been heard a hundred
times from others. "Listen, why does he think I always
have to be the one to get up when the baby cries at
night?"

Volodya came home after eleven. He wanted to sit and
talk with us, but he had an exam in the morning and had

to study. He spread out his books, and Tanya and I went into the kitchen. Ten minutes later, Tanya glanced into the room and beckoned to me with her finger: Volodya's head lay on his books and he was sleeping.

She wakened him and said, "Tomorrow, you stay with the baby. I have to study for my English exam."

"No," he replied, "I've already missed so many classes. How come you don't understand that my plans to get into graduate school are melting away."

"And how is it you don't understand that for me everything is melting away!"

From WE THE RUSSIANS: Voices from Russia edited by Colette Shulman, p. 189. © 1971 by Praeger Publishers, Inc. New York. Excerpted and reprinted by permission.

When he got his pay, Slava often went out drinking with his friends, not because he enjoyed drinking but because he could not say no. Irina, of course, objected, and it wasn't at all for the sake of saving money—the reader will soon understand this. At first, she went to the factory entrance, where many of the women gathered, and accompanied her husband home. Their friends laughed, as one might expect, and Irina wept and started noisy quarrels in front of everyone, on the staircase, yelling at the top of her voice. She was, as Maria Osipovna put it, "a decent girl, but bold." And the neighbors, as everyone knows, are capable of adding ten words of their own to every word they hear. The whole family really felt for Slava and his shaky honor. He calmed his wife down as best he could and said to her, "Don't scream, people are listening," but it made no difference—she was a real "Italian" type. "To hell with them" she would scream. "You are the one I care about."

However long or short a time this went on, by the time I got to know the Polyanovs, a "new life" had already triumphed in their family. On the day he got his pay, Slava put on a white shirt and a bright tie, well pressed (by him, I note in parentheses), gray trousers, a brown jacket with a beige handkerchief jutting out of the pocket, black loafers whose heels he had had cut into a conical shape—at Irina's insistence—and, together with his wife, who put on a little lipstick, went off to a restaurant.

Boris Yefimovich—Slava's father—contemptuously called the restaurant a "'restoratsia' where gilded ladies walk around practically naked." He just couldn't understand that a restaurant is not necessarily a place to get drunk in, that it can be a place where you listen to music, dance, look at people, and are seen by them. Watching his son leave, he peered at him over the top of his glasses as if to say that his son had fallen so low he had hit rock bottom.

Today in Slava's family there is "no division between man and woman," as Irina put it. It was hard to achieve that; it meant breaking with character and tradition, yet Irina achieved it, and now she and her husband do everything together—they go out on the town together, and keep house and look after their daughter together. While Slava did the marketing, Irina hammered a metal cornice into the wall. She did it badly, of course, but even here they were equal, since the dinners that Slava prepared were sometimes oversalted. Never mind, they ate them and laughed. It is interesting that Slava did not conceal his kitchen concerns from his neighbors. He walked proudly and did not attempt to hide the string bag he carried out of the Deluxe, as the nearest store was called. He considered equality to be fair and just, because he had learned a simple truth: If you do good to your wife, life will be better for you.

Do you hear this, men?

SPAIN AND LATIN AMERICA. Of all European countries, present-day Spain is the most traditional with respect to the status of women (20). Young women are forbidden by law to leave their fathers' homes except to get married or to enter a nunnery. A married woman cannot hold a job, open a bank account, apply for a passport, sign a legal contract, or obtain legal custody of her children without her husband's written permission. A wife who is found guilty of adultery can be sent to prison, but men are not penalized, legally or otherwise, for their infidelities.

The machismo norm is still quite prevalent in Spain, although apparently less than in Latin America. Boys and men who are raised in this tradition value sexual conquest very strongly. Exaggerated toughness and bravery are also part of the machismo ideal. These values are believed to have been brought to Spain by the Moorish conquerors, who occupied Spain between the tenth and the fourteenth centuries. From Spain the machismo pattern was transported to Latin America by the Conquistadores. The conquered female Indian population provided ample premarital and extramarital sexual outlets for the Spanish rulers. The pattern flourished and became even stronger in Latin America than in Spain and Portugal (21).

The Catholic church provided strong reinforcement for certain patriarchal attitudes, although it did not condone sexual liberalism for the male. The church, here as elsewhere, defined women as property and as childbearers, as exalted madonnas (the mother image) and as evil temptresses (the Eve image). The ideal female, mother or wife, was humble, virtuous, pious, submissive, and long suffering.

The civil codes of most Latin American countries contain a provision called *patria potestas*. This law gives the husband absolute authority and automatic power of attorney over his wife. A husband can dispose of his wife's property without her consent. The absence of legal divorce deprives the wife of escape in the case of abuse or exploitation. The philosophic rationale for *patria potestas* rests on the doctrine of *imbecilus sexus*—the view of women as weak, helpless, and stupid. Legally, women have the status of immature children and retardates.

Ironically, this doctrine has resulted in certain progressive policies lacking in countries such as the United States. In many Latin American countries, women cannot be fired because of pregnancy. They receive paid maternity leaves before and after delivery. Obstetrical care is free, and many large factories and firms are required to provide day nurseries and time off for nursing to their female employees.

Until recently, and even now in rural areas of Spain, Portugal, and Latin America, women were rigidly chaperoned. Premarital virginity was a sacred standard for all classes. The dual requirement of both civil and religious ceremonies to legalize a marriage is believed to underlie the widespread existence of the consensual union (*union libre*), or common-law marriage, in Latin America. The pattern is promoted by the expense of two ceremonies and also by the absence of clergy in many rural areas. Although there are no strong sanctions against consensual unions in lower income groups, it is not a preferred pattern. This is indicated quite clearly by in-depth studies of family life by investigators such as Oscar Lewis (22). The practice is much less frequent within the middle classes, where women are less willing to tolerate it.

Machismo persists in Latin America, particularly but not exclusively among lower income groups. Machismo values encourage consensual unions. Masculine virility continues to be defined in terms of fertility. The machismo pattern declines, however, in the middle class, where more and more the male defines his masculinity in terms of economic achievements. The support of two households and many children interferes with getting ahead.

The trend just described has been documented for Mexican-Americans in the United States recently (23). Middle class Mexican-American males, who live outside the barrios in large urban centers, are much more apt to validate their masculinity in terms of achievement than through sexual conquest. At the same time, their wives—more educated, more equalitarian, and less fatalistic—are less accepting of the traditional pattern.

The traditional value of familism, still quite strong in Latin America, tends to reinforce machismo norms, sex typing, and the segregation of the sexes. Urbanization is proceeding faster than industrialization. Relatives often settle together in the slums that circle most large Latin American cities, and the exchange of daily services between migrant extended families continues as in the villages. The migrants, who come in search of the opportunities they did not have as subsistence or tenant farmers, encounter unemployment and severe poverty. Fathers desert. Many mothers work as servants or semiskilled factory laborers, even while their children are infants. It is not uncommon, in the early morning hours, to see a woman carrying her young infant to a relative or neighbor. The child is left until evening, when the mother returns from work. The same scene is repeated on the streets of Spanish Harlem in New York, every weekday morning.

Aside from the objective lack of economic opportunity in most industrializing Latin American countries, the persistence of authoritarianism in childrearing both discourages achievement motivation in males and reinforces machismo behavior. Mothers are afraid to set high standards for their sons, whose success might be viewed as a threat by the patriarchal father. This pattern is not uncommon in traditional societies that are in the process of change.

Extreme sex typing is promoted by the rigid separation of the sexes in all spheres of living. Where virginity is sanctified, even among the poor, the segregation of the sexes is difficult to break down. This is a major reason for the sex typing of jobs in all societies. It is feared that contact between the sexes at work will lead to premarital or extramarital relationships.

Nevertheless, many women have entered the professions and administrative work in Latin America. Well-educated, urban, upper middle class women, here as elsewhere, have led the way. And to some extent the pattern has touched the lives of upper class women, who everywhere have been the most protected and secluded in agricultural societies. As a rule, the shortage of men with high levels of skill and education has promoted such opportunities for women, although the absolute number of these jobs in industrializing countries is relatively small. However, most women work in manual jobs—by far the largest sector in developing countries.

The women's movement in Latin America is barely functioning. More highly educated women do not experience gross discrimination in an economy that needs them. And the masses of Latin American women are too isolated and too traditional to be reached by women's movement leaders.

Highly educated, urban women in Latin America limit the size of their families, but not simply because their educational experiences have taught them the modern values—rationalism, individualism, and equalitarianism, especially. In urban areas, less educated women who are gainfully employed continue to have traditional values and high fertility rates (24). The kind of work that women do, which in modern society depends on education rather than physical strength or other biological characteristics, is more important than work, per se, for changing attitudes and values.

The masses of women in Latin America live in isolated rural environments. They are illiterate; intensely religious and fatalistic; they are ethnocentric, and they are deeply submerged within the patriarchal family structure.

The persistence of traditional values in rural Latin America is illustrated in the following episodes reported in *Five Families*. This book is based on tape-recorded interviews and lengthy observations of the day-to-day life of five families in different stages of acculturation to the modern values. It is a remarkable document of the conflict and suffering of men and women who have experienced the great changes wrought by industrialization and urbanization. The first excerpt documents patriarchalism and the nature of the marital tie in a description of a past courtship and marriage in a rural village near Mexico City. The wife's low self esteem and submissiveness represent a theme that recurs throughout the book.

Esperanza had never learned to read or write and could
not defend herself when Pedro accused her of being igno-
rant and stupid. But she would say, "Didn't you know
what I was when you sent your mother to ask for me?"
Indeed, when Pedro had looked about for a wife he had
decided that the young Eperanza, who was virtuous and
innocent and poorer than he, was the ideal girl for him.
Esperanza had not wanted to marry him or anyone else,
but when his mother died and he was left an orphan with
no one to make his *tortillas*, she took pity on him and
consented.

A few days before the marriage her mother had given her
advice: "Now that you are going to marry you must have
a different character. Here you have one character but
there you must have the character of your husband. If he
scolds you, do not answer. If he beats you, bear it because
if not your husband is going to say, 'What kind of up-
bringing did we give?'" Esperanza had followed her
mother's advice. "And I was always that way," she
thought. "When Pedro hit me I only sat down and cried."

The marriage took place in the village church in 1910.
Pedro gave Esperanza the first dress she had ever had
(before that she had always worn a blouse and long skirt).
He gave her a fifty centavo piece to spend. He took her
to live with him and his aunt in his one-room house.

"I remember the night we married. I was terribly afraid.
Pedro still bothers me sometimes when he says jokingly,
'Why were you so frightened that night?' In reality I do
not know what it was that troubled me. Chills came over
me. I was terribly afraid, for never, never had we spoken
to one another. After we ate dinner Pedro's aunt went to
bed and so did he. He had gone to bed with his clothes
on. He has always done that. I also always go to bed with
my clothes on. The aunt told me that for this I had got
married and that I should go to bed. I was very afraid
and ashamed. Pedro covered me with the blanket and
then began to embrace me and touch my breasts. Then
he went on top of me. I didn't know what the men did to
one, and I said to myself, 'Maybe it's like this.' I felt like
crying or going to my mother, but I remembered that
they had married me and then I said, 'If I die, I'll die. I
have to go through with it here even though he kills me.'

And I closed my eyes and waited for the worst. Pedro already know how these things were done because he had even had a daughter by a married woman. I don't remember that I bled, but I know that it hurt a lot, and I didn't cry because there was someone else there and it would make me ashamed if she heard.

"Two weeks later I was still afraid. Little by little one picks up confidence. I didn't even tell anything to my mother. I only told a cousin of my husband. I said: 'Men only play with one. Why do they have to get married?' Then she said, 'That's the way they are and you have to let him.' After about two months I was feeling pleasure and then I began to love my husband."

From pp. 48–49 in FIVE FAMILIES: Mexican Case Studies in the Culture of Poverty, by Oscar Lewis, © 1959 by Basic Books, Inc., Publishers, New York.

In another episode from the lives of the same couple, we see the persistence of the traditional values of fatalism, religiosity, and superstition in the mother's reaction to her son's illness. The father affirms the machismo values of stoicism and fortitude. The struggle between familistic values and individual desire is demonstrated in the conflict between father and son over the son's desire to marry.

Pedro and Esperanza sat near the fire occasionally saying something in a low voice. "Do you have money for tomorrow?" asked Pedro. "Who knows if it will be enough?" Esperanza said. They heard the sound of coughing in the other room. "Richardo has a cough," said Esperanza. "I'll rub his chest with alcohol." She took the bottle and went into the boys' room. A few minutes later she came out. "He says that his lungs hurt. His body is hot. I think the spirits have hit him." Esperanza was worried; for her, illness in the family was always a serious matter. She had given birth to twelve children and only six were alive. Their first child had died at eight "of the stomach," the second at eight months of smallpox, the third at two of

a scorpion bite. Later two more children, aged seven
and three, died "of the stomach." The last child, a daughter born in 1940, had died at ten months of "bronchitis."

Pedro was impatient with his wife. "It's a little thing.
Don't make a woman out of him. Just give him some
lemon tea and he will be better by tomorrow."

Esperanza stirred up the dying fire and put on the
water to boil. She took a candle out with her into the garden and after groping about for a moment came back
with a few blades of lemon grass which she dropped into
the water. When the tea was ready she added some
drinking alcohol and took it to her son. "That will cure
him," Pedro said when she returned. But Esperanza said,
"He has chills now. Let him stay in bed tomorrow. He is
barely eighteen and still but a boy." Pedro looked at her
with annoyance. "Be quiet!" he said. "What do you know,
woman? When I was ten, I was working like a man, supporting my mother and my sister. He must learn what it
means to be a man."

At nine-thirty Felipe walked in. His father said, "Now
you are here." Felipe nodded and went to bed. He had
never been one to talk much, but for the past two weeks
he hadn't addressed a word to his father. "He is angry
again," observed Esperanza. "Who knows why?" Pedro
knew why. It was because of the girl in Mexico City
whom Felipe had decided he wanted to marry. He had
met the girl only once for a few moments when he and
his father had gone to the city to arrange for a sale of
plums. She was an Aztecan girl but she had gone to
school in Mexico City and was now a "lady of fashion."
She wore shoes and stockings all the time and had cut off
her braids. But she had smiled at Felipe and although he
was a poor country boy he had dared to hope that she
liked him. Felipe did not sleep well for a whole week
after he had seen her. Finally he had asked his father to
arrange the marriage with the girl's family.

Pedro had been against it from the start. "Think well,"
he had argued. "She lives in the city and we don't know
her habits. She might even be a street woman and we
wouldn't know." Pedro had really been taken aback by

Felipe's request. Nowadays young people arranged their own marriages in secret before their parents were called in to carry out the traditional steps. If the parents objected the young couple usually eloped and made peace with their families later. But Felipe, who had never been fortunate with girls, did not smooth out the path for his father, and Pedro, although he had agreed to ask for the girl's hand, kept putting it off. Sometimes he growled at Felipe, "Do you still want to marry that girl in Mexico City?" He succeeded in turning the whole thing into a joke and Felipe was furious. So now the boy wouldn't speak to his father at all.

Pedro did not mind. The financial burden of the wedding, the gifts to the bride and her family, the support of his daughter-in-law while Felipe lived with them—all this would be more than he could manage. In the old days a son might live on with his father and more than repay these expenses by working for him, but nowadays young couples generally moved away after a year, leaving the parents with all their debts. The worst blow of all would be to lose a good worker. So Pedro kept his sons under close watch and saw to it that they worked hard and did not spend much time in the streets with the other young men. He discouraged them from thinking of having a good time or spending money on clothes, diversions, or other vanities.

From pp. 62–64 in FIVE FAMILIES: Mexican Case Studies in the Culture of Poverty, by Oscar Lewis, © 1959 by Basic Books, Inc., Publishers, New York.

At the opposite end of the traditional-to-modern continuum seemingly, would be the life of a wealthy, upper middle class woman living in Mexico City. She is educated, and she enjoys the latest in material comfort. And yet she accepts the beatings, infidelities, and humiliations meted out to her by a traditional, authoritarian husband. Communication is poor, companionship is limited, and psychological support is absent:

David backed the car toward the gate. He drove with great aplomb and was soon lost to sight at the end of the street. Isabel stood looking in the direction he had gone. Her husband puzzled her. She truthfully could not tell whether he loved her or hated her. Sometimes he was pleasant and affectionate, "so sweet he swallows me in one gulp." But at other times he was brutal and took pleasure in belittling her. He made her beg for money, he struck her with little provocation, and he flaunted himself before her as a Don Juan. He had once gone so far as to ask her to give him an injection which she discovered to be testosterone, a male hormone that he took to stimulate his sexual powers. Since he made sexual demands of her only once a month, she knew he must be taking the hormone "so that he could be more of a man with his sweetheart." She was so angry that she jabbed him too hard and the needle broke and had to be removed by surgery.

Isabel complained that she could never have a discussion with David because he insisted that he was always right and did not think her opinions worth listening to. "He never gives me credit for the things I do well. He never makes me feel secure." Whenever she took an interest in his personal or business affairs or expressed tenderness for him, she would be rebuffed. "It is as though he has a barrier around him which he lets no one penetrate."

Isabel believed David tried to isolate her from the society of people she enjoyed. In the past they had invited guests to dinners and parties at their home and Isabel had often been asked to play the guitar. "But," she said, "David couldn't bear to hear people compliment me and didn't want parties any more." She had had to give up her friends and was limited to visiting only her own family. She often went to the movies and did a great deal of shopping. It was now many years since she had played the instrument.

Occasionally David would take her with him when he went out with his friends, most of whom were businessmen and politicians. He liked to go to night clubs or to expensive restaurants and thought nothing of footing the bill for everyone. Isabel had seen him spend as much as two thousand pesos in one evening. He also spent as much betting on bull fights and baseball, his favorite sports. With friends he drank heavily and became noisy and aggressive. He liked to wrestle and had a trick of embracing some friend tightly and then lifting him up from the floor to show the strength of his arms. He had once cracked a friend's ribs doing this.

Isabel had at one time tried to improve David's manners and taste, "to civilize him," as she put it. Although she had had no training in the arts, she enjoyed them and urged her husband to take her to the opera and the theater, to concerts and art galleries. These "cultural" outings bored David, however, and he put a stop to them.

From pp. 282–283 in FIVE FAMILIES: Mexican Case Studies in the Culture of Poverty, by Oscar Lewis, © 1959 by Basic Books, Inc., Publishers, New York.

THE ARAB MIDDLE EAST.   In a few countries in the Middle East the women's movement has been seeking to alter the status of women at least since the 1920s, but with little success. Since the wave of political revolutions that shook much of the region in the 1950s, government policy in most Arabic nations has had the same goal: largely through promoting education for women, Arab governments have hoped to bring women into the economy as a necessary force in industrial development.

Deliberately and systematically, political leaders have sought to change popular values—to emphasize achievement motivation for both sexes and to alleviate problems, such as very high fertility rates, which hamper economic development. High fertility rates slow industrial growth because resources must be channeled into feeding large populations rather than into building factories.

In keeping with the goal of changing traditional values and expanding political, educational, and economic opportunities, women have been given the right to vote in a number of Middle Eastern (and near Eastern) countries—although usually with qualifications that are not applied to men. Clitoridectomy has been outlawed in Egypt. Polygyny is frowned on, particularly among the urban middle classes, and the right of the male to divorce his wife at whim has been curtailed. Equal and free interaction between men and women is increasing. Educational teams have been sent into the countryside as part of large-scale efforts (nowhere near adequate to the need) to teach women the rudiments of sanitation, health care, contraception, and good nutrition (25). Rural women have been taught how to prepare a salad, make soap, and wash their children to prevent infection. They have been taught simple crafts that have market value in the industrial economy. Taught to read, write, and count, now they can read labels on cans and count change when they go marketing. Eventually they will be able to read newspapers and develop a national consciousness.

Literacy was not important to women in traditional Arab societies, since they rarely left their fields and their houses. Men had the contacts with the outside world, particularly when they did the marketing. This task was denied to women in keeping with the standard of female seclusion. Men totally controlled all economic resources of the family, including whatever money was earned by the labor of the wife.

Now more and more husbands are working in factories, offices, and stores. Boys, increasingly, are in school, as are girls. Women must do the marketing, since no one else is available. They are coming out, slowly and steadily.

Rural women in the market place may encounter city-bred women whose husbands have been sent to fill local government posts or to assume jobs as managers in the small industrial plants that are beginning to dot the countryside (26). They observe the dress, speech, and behavior of the more highly educated, more sophisticated women. They notice that the middle class, educated families who have come to live among them do things together. Husband and wife go to movies and restaurants together. The husband does not spend long hours with his male friends in the coffee shops (substitute pub, club, or bar in other countries). Couples walk arm in arm in public, joking with each other and laughing. The local citizens, men and women, identify with this new class. Their values and self conceptions begin to change. Fatalism declines. Women begin to view themselves as acting rather than acted upon—as having a voice in determining their destinies: "It will be God's will, but I can also help" (27).

Television also provides new models. The local school often serves as a center for viewing the single television set in the village. Horizons are broadened, new ideas are spread, and new ambitions are born (28).

And yet the process of modernization is slow—far slower in the realm of values than in the material sphere. A majority of men who have been surveyed in various Arab countries feel that women should not work in the industrial economy under any circumstances, especially if they are married. Older women tend to agree.

Everywhere in the Middle East, this attitude is largely explained by the conflict between family and job obligations that gainful employment involves. Neglect of children is most feared, particularly with the decline of the extended family and in the absence of adequate day care centers. The possibility that unsanctioned sexual relationships will occur is also a grave source of trouble to Arab men, who attribute strong erotic drives to women. Finally, the threat to masculinity and to male authority is cited in objections to outside employment for women.

The same reasons for opposing gainful employment of married women are given by men in highly industrialized nations also, especially in the working class. The fear of possible infidelity or promiscuity on the part of the employed wife is less strong (or less conscious), however, in countries where women are not believed to be more highly endowed than men with erotic desires. It is also less strong where women have free choice in obtaining marital partners and are more likely to have married for love.

Ambivalence in attitudes toward women prevails in Islamic as well as in Christian cultures. In Egypt, for example, and in modernizing black African nations (both with a tradition in which women have often been more economically productive than men), highly educated and skilled women are greatly valued (29). They bring higher bride prices, where this practice still exists, particularly in sub-Saharan Africa. It is recognized that the economic contributions of educated women to the family budget can be considerable and desirable. Middle class males also value an educated wife for the intellectual companionship she can provide. This attitude appears to be spreading in all countries, modernizing and modern, particularly as companionship between husband and wife is increasingly valued. Ambivalence and inconsistencies persist, however. A recent study of college males in the United States revealed that the young men wanted strong, competent, resourceful, intelligent, and highly educated wives. At the same time, however, they expected that their wives would stay home and play the traditional role after the children were born (30).

Women continue to make very significant contributions to production in agriculture in Arab countries. They sow seeds, clear weeds, prepare and carry fuel, tend domesticated animals, and help with house building. Their importance to the agricultural economy also discourages their employment in the industrial sector. The majority of women who are employed in the industrial sector are young and unmarried, and their numbers are heavily concentrated in less skilled occupations. Good day care centers are almost nonexistent. Educational opportunities, while increasing, still discriminate against girls and women, since males are taught first when there is a shortage of classrooms and teachers. Where they have the right to vote, women are less likely than men to exercise this right. And when they do, they vote as their husbands do—even for conservative candidates who radically oppose women's rights.

It is not unusual for children of both sexes to be pulled out of school to help with homemaking or agricultural chores, particularly during harvest time. Mothers are often suspicious of modern clinics or hospitals, and if a child is ill, they are still likely to fall back on religious or magical practices to effect a cure. Rationalism comes hard to the illiterate and the fatalistic.

Women generally, however, are shifting very gradually toward the modern values; educated women faster than less educated women, urban women more frequently than rural women. Education is the keystone of this change. Middle class parents are investing in the security of academic degrees for their daughters as well as their sons, under rapidly changing and unpredictable social conditions.

The majority of Arabs are still rural and illiterate. However, the general direction of change in the identities and relative status of women and men is the same as in all urbanized, industrialized societies, whatever the pace, and however much the pattern varies in detail.

The following is a selection from the memoirs of an Iranian woman. Educated for several years in the United States, she returned to Persia to teach. The eagerness to learn, the clash between the old and the new, and the submerged identity of Iranian women is revealed in this excerpt. The lack of a term meaning "wife" in the Iranian language indicates the diffuse identity of traditional women in this society.

> On October 18, the work-study room was clean and ready for the women's classes to begin. I had brought a bell from Teheran and this I struck; its resounding voice echoed through the valley. Asghar took the megaphone from its nail in the bathhouse and called, "School today. School today!"
>
> We, the girls and I, had been talking quietly about this school as we went on our calls through the village. Now from the little houses the girls and women came in a broken stream. In the first hour there were sixty-eight who had registered. Sixty-eight! I had planned on thirty, or thirty-five at the most. I had not read the real hunger for

learning that was behind the women's noncommittal comments whenever the school had been mentioned.

Working in Sarbandan was like climbing Mt. Damavand. Every time I reached the top of the "last" hill, another rose before me.

The answer to my overcrowded classroom was to find and furnish a school for the little girls so that in my school I could teach the mothers and the older girls. I put this problem to the back of my mind for further consideration while I began that first difficult day.

The smell in the little room grew to be an all-pervading stench. Sixty-eight unwashed bodies, sixty-eight pairs of unwashed bare feet.

Again, with all my high plans for the school, I had to begin at the very bottom. "Look at your feet. Are they clean?" So after all, the first lesson that was taught in the new schoolroom was one in simple cleanliness. "You must wash your feet each day before you come to school."

"We shall have two sessions of school," I told them. "In the morning the children and the younger girls; in the afternoon the women and the older girls."

I didn't want the women and children together because the conversation of the women was not appropriate for the children to hear. Morning would be the best time for the women to clean their houses, bring in their water and wood, take care of their few animals. In the afternoon the children could mind the babies while the mother was gone.

The women and the older girls left, the younger girls and the children stayed. From my school supplies I took out unusual materials—combs and kerosene. With the help of Farkhondeh and Effat I began the lesson. There was not a girl in the room whose hair was not peopled with tiny lice—lice loved to live in clay houses. We dipped a comb in kerosene, combed out the lice, wiped the comb on paper, dipped it again, combed again, dipped again. It seemed an endless job with the forty girls wiggling protestingly under the scraping combs. As we worked I explained about the lice, showed them what the lice were like, how to recognize the nits. Then I talked with them about being clean. We would learn many things in the school, I promised, but first we must be clean. . . .

. . . . When I had first begun to teach good grooming in my classes, angry fathers came to me: "What are you trying to do to my daughter? Make her to be a prostitute?" For in Iran the women who sell their bodies to the wealthy are some of the most carefully kept women. Now good grooming, neat dressing, soft speaking, personal cleanliness were expected and enjoyed. Men were beginning to think of their women as something more than docile mates. This was a great step forward. In the village there is no word for *wife*. The village man uses the same word to mean both wife and home. Or he may call his wife by the name of his first son. This habit of speech, alone, shows the position of women. No man can say, "I love my wife," or "I respect my wife." Yet I felt a change. Someday the men could say these things.

SUB–SAHARAN AFRICA. Women in sub-Saharan Africa experience many of the disabilities and problems that change has brought to women in all modernizing countries. They are losing their traditional, family-based forms of security, and they are not receiving adequate government and community support for the new choices that become possible with industrialization. Despite great variations within Africa, however, women generally share certain advantages over most of their compatriots in other industrializing countries. Most have a long history of economic independence. They have traditionally performed basic food producing functions, and they have usually controlled the resources they produced. They have also monopolized craft production and trading in many societies. Even in the Muslim areas of sub-Saharan Africa, where veiling and the purdah have been practiced, unmarried women and postmenopausal women have engaged in trade (31).

Many African women, especially in matrilineal societies, have had more sexual freedom than is typical in traditional preindustrial societies. The shortage of population in Africa, a product largely of very high death rates, has also enhanced the status of women for their childbearing capacities.

Most of the foregoing differences are traceable to the survival into modern times of horticultural societies in Africa. The agricultural era has been relatively short, having been imposed in many societies by European conquerors. It did not last long enough for strong patriarchal attitudes to develop, particularly where the base was a matrilineal society.

Practices that are associated with subsistence economic roles for women—polygyny and the bride price—were and are widespread in Africa. Here as in other societies, however, most adults lived in monogamous households.

It is not surprising that the mythical Amazon society was supposed to have existed in Africa, where woman's status has been higher than in traditional agricultural societies. Yet no one, neither anthropologist nor amateur traveler, has unearthed any evidence of a society ruled by Amazon women—a true matriarchy. What did exist, in Dahomey, between the seventeenth and nineteenth centuries and until the French occupation, was a society ruled by a male king, who recruited an Amazon warrior corps of women to serve under him (32). Recruited as young girls, these women were required to remain virgins. They received training identical to that of male warriors. They took on the personality, traits, and skills of their male associates, and apparently identified themselves as males. Other women in Dahomey society also occupied high positions of power, but as advisors and functionaries in service of the king—who was the ultimate authority.

A number of other tribes in sub-Saharan Africa have had women chiefs, on occasion. And often a male chief's mother or sister exercised independent authority over women in the society, exacting separate tribute and presiding over women's affairs.

Women in certain sub-Saharan African societies also have a long history of organizing into interest groups or associations—craft guilds, and more recently, mutual benefit associations, trade associations, self-improvement clubs, and international organizations. In the early days of European occupation, many women operated through their organizations to protest against the colonizing powers. They revolted against taxes imposed on their property. They fought against the loss of status they often experienced when colonial governments created new occupations in agriculture and in local government from which they were excluded (33).

Colonial governments upset the previous balance of authority between men and women by providing new educational as well as occupational resources for males only. They set up schools to train men in agricultural production, in trade, and in administration. They established plantations, mines, factories, and commercial facilities that utilized male talents and energies. The education of women was relegated to Christian missionaries who concentrated more on instilling Western Christian morality than on improving the economic skills of women.

African women have approached the changes of modernization starting with a higher status than has been typical for women in agricultural societies. They have responded to the effects of urbanization and industrialization differently. To begin, many women who have followed their husbands or other relatives to the cities have experienced a decline in status. They are no longer food producers, and they are not employable in jobs in the urban economy that require literacy.

Males far outnumber females in urban areas. On the one hand, this has always raised the status of women (e.g., in colonial and frontier America), but it also promotes prostitution and com-

mon-law marital arrangements. Such arrangements are tolerated
in most urban cultures of poverty in industrializing societies,
but they are not preferred, by women at least. Women who are
more educated and more economically independent are less
willing to accept common-law relationships. In urban Africa,
however, male extramarital liaisons have been reinforced by survivals of polygynous traditions. Actual polygyny is rare in urban
areas, particularly among the educated middle classes, but tolerance of male infidelity is greater in all classes than is typical in
European countries.

Women have also had unusual freedom in the sexual sphere,
however, especially women who come from matrilineal societies,
where the child is the property of the mother's clan. Thus with
children belonging to the mother's side, and given the shortage
of population, biological paternity has not been as great a concern as in patriarchal, agricultural societies. In fact, as one investigator has observed, while illegitimacy was rare in traditional agricultural societies, families fought over the right to,
rather than the responsibility for, an illegitimate child (34).

Certain familistic patterns in traditional Africa that weighed
heavily on women (e.g., infant betrothal of girls to older males)
were abolished by the colonizing powers. Polygyny was disapproved of but tolerated. These patterns persist, but tribal customs continue to change in the direction of European patterns,
faster in some countries than in others.

Industrialization and increased urbanization have reinforced
the changes just mentioned. Tribal influences are declining rapidly, particularly among the uprooted men and women who live
and work in the cities. Extended families are often unable to
settle in the same neighborhood because of housing shortages.
The nuclear family, more or less isolated from relatives, and
freer from their control, is becoming common.

Freedom of choice in marriage is spreading, particularly
among more educated women in the cities. Africa, too, is gradually converting to the pattern that tends to become typical in
all modernizing nations in which seclusion of women has not

been extreme. Young women increasingly choose their own marital partners. They usually inform their parents, who, if they consent, then make the necessary arrangements. In the more disorganized parts of southern Africa, however, parents are often not informed until after the marriage has taken place—a practice that is atypical even in the most highly industrialized societies. Young people who do not consult their parents at all can manage with jobs in the nonfamily economy, but they risk cutting off all future help from their families, particularly in emergencies. However, the separation of migrating young women from their elders, and the higher levels of education and the greater earning power in the industrial economy of younger generations of urban women, increase women's independence and freedom of choice.

The background of African women in some ways hinders and in some ways promotes their acculturation to modern values. The technological gap is often wider than in other industrializing countries. Ideologically, however, the African woman's age-old economic independence and resourcefulness is almost unparalleled. The large network of voluntary associations, now mainly concerned with providing aid to migrating women, could eventually serve as a base for encouraging a more active role in government and greater representation in higher level administrative jobs for African women.

Two accounts of different reactions toward the persistence of polygyny by contemporary, rural Nigerian women illustrate the differences in acculturation of women as this phenomenon relates to class. The first woman, from a very wealthy family, desires to preserve the secure forms of the past. She approves of polygyny and depends very strongly on her children and her extended family:

> It is a good thing for a woman when the husband has more than one wife. The wife will not have regular visits to other men's wives which perhaps might not create an impression to the husband of such women. When a

woman has many co-wives, her own children will have many brothers and sisters of the same father to play with, instead of going outside to create some troubles with other people's children. By having many co-wives, one will learn to be social with her co-wives and children will grow up to copy how their mothers lived in peace, co-operation and sociality with her co-wives.

My last sister has been most considerate to me. It does not mean that she has been giving me many things, but she takes me as her real mother. She visits me as she should do to either my mother or my father who died. She does not have any discrimination on my own children, rather she takes them as her own children as well. I value more her good manners than a fat sum of money she could give to me.

Now I am above the age of having friends outside my family, rather I have my children as my friends. My children are the people helping me both in finance and otherwise. They care very well about my good health. I do not help them in any way because I was the one maintaining them till they grew up to be responsible people. They are now expected to help me in any way possible as I am getting weak and older.

My life has been a different one from that of my mother because I have got trained children who educate me on how to live to suit with the present way of life. I enjoy more delicious food than my mother did. I dress in a better and neatful way than she did and enjoy many more improvements in life than my mother did.

Indeed, life has got better these days than the days I was young because of highly qualified men and women who helped to bring in civilization into our village. People are made to understand anything that is worth doing more than it was in days gone by. People have freedom to do anything they feel will be of benefit to them.

A second Nigerian woman, from humbler circumstances, is more disapproving of traditional forms such as polygyny:

To the best of my knowledge, I say it is always a bad thing for a woman when the husband has more than one wife. There has never been any peace in a polygamous family. In days gone by, men who married many wives were often regarded as the most richest men. Women whose husbands married many wives often enjoyed the married home because they were not so much after luxuries as the modern women. The depended wholly and entirely on their farms, while the modern women are depending on their husbands. These are some of the reasons that many wives find it difficult to make a happy home in a polygamous family.

I have no friend outside my family. My children are the people who are now kindest to me. They do everything within their power to make me forget about my late brothers, sisters and relatives, who passed away during the last influenza attack.

I don't confide with anybody else other than my children. And they have satisfied me more than others could do. If any of them comes from his or her station, I usually cook for them. I also help in nursing their children as well as their mother would do. Immediately their children are up to one year, I always asked the parents to send them to me so that the children might be familiar with me.

My life is different from that of my parents in dressing, the way of behaving, eating delicious foods, and knowing what is good and that which is bad. Things moved very slow and backward but now civilization makes things very simple and plain.

Reprinted by permission of Schocken Books Inc. from *Old Wives' Tales* by Iris Andreski. Copyright © 1970 Iris Andreski, pp. 110–111, p. 168.

African males have experienced detribalization with varying reactions. One Bantu male speaks of his longing for the traditional life and his abhorrence of materialistic values. A second African male, from Nyasaland, who has taken to a wandering existence, bemoans his rootlessness—a condition that is underwritten by his lack of acquisitiveness. The men grew up in subsistence societies. In the absence of trade and gross differences in wealth, materialism and acquisitiveness are irrelevant to most subsistence economies, and these men have not made the shift to the new values.

I have no wish to be turned into a black white man, or a white black man, not for all the money in the Reserve Bank. I do not wish to live the kind of life the white man leads—a life of tension, fear, and ceaseless worry, of competition and rivalry, a life of selfish ambition and of "doing unto others before they do unto you." I do not want to strip myself of all human feelings, moral standards, of conscience itself, to sell body and soul to the spirit of money. I do not want ulcers or coronary thrombosis. Nor do I want my children to be soulless half-breeds dressed in jeans, rocking and rolling to the Beatles morning, noon and night, and calling me "Daddy-O."

All I ask of life is to be granted the opportunity to live again in a typical Zulu kraal, at peace with the world, with a Bantu wife to bear me stalwart Bantu sons and daughters to whom I can teach the tribal law and in whom I can instill respect and reverence for our tribal heritage, and no squads of policemen raiding me in the small hours of the night to check where I was born and whether I have a permit to be where I am.

I was walking on the road, a dusty road just like the one at home. On both sides of the road were trees. They stood tall and thick as far as they went. I was walking on this dusty road; really, with most of my toes bleeding, I was hobbling. Once in a while I would look back at my footprints, and I would grieve to myself that these footprints would soon be washed away by the water of rain, or they would soon be swept away by the broom of wind, and more grieving was the thought that my mother

would never come here and see these footprints and say,
"I know who passed here" . . . .

. . . . Once I met my bicycle friend. After getting over
the surprise of finding me there when he thought I was
piling up mileage elsewhere, he invited me to visit him
whenever I could. I did one Sunday afternoon, riding on
his bicycle with the man who had come to pick me up. It
was an interesting evening, talking what politics we knew
under the same kerosene lamp, and consuming cups of
tea with scones while the wireless blasted forth Tangan-
yika music interrupted occasionally by the voice of a
news announcer.

To one who has taken to wandering from place to
place, from country to country, and to whom meeting
new faces has become a common thing and making new
acquaintances a routine, a good living once established
survives only until the impulse to wandering revives. And
when the wandering has a purpose, pleasures acquired at
any stopping place must be forfeited. They can, one
hopes, be acquired just as easily at any stopping place
elsewhere if one remembers how one acquired them at
any given stopping place. When the need for a cement
and sand mixer disappears, and when the bricks have all
been wheeled to their final place, a stranded man such as
I departs and strikes once more for the distant destina-
tion.

Excerpts from I WILL TRY by Legson Kayira, p. 94, p.
135. Copyright © by Legson Kayira. Reprinted by permission of Harold Matson Co., Inc.

TECHNOLOGY AND IDEOLOGY. My brief discussion of
sexual identity in various parts of the world has illustrated how
new or preexisting political and religious ideologies have tempered the effects of technological development. The roles, identities, personalities, and relationships of men and women around
the world have not changed (in the short run, at least) only and

in direct relation to technological development and advances in scientific knowledge.

In countries that have adopted very conservative political ideologies—fascism, for example—changes in the role and status of women have been reversed or delayed. The success of National Socialism in Germany during the 1930s resulted in a shift back toward more traditional conceptions of masculinity and femininity. More extreme status distinctions between the sexes arose, despite continued industrialization. In the days of the Weimar Republic, prior to the victory of the Nazis, the Social Democrats had made some effort to extend the horizons of German women beyond the Kinder–Küche–Kirche (children–kitchen–church) model. The universities, the professions, and the German bureaucracy were open to them to a greater extent than ever before.

The "new woman" emerged in the 1920s, in Germany, as well as in the United States and elsewhere. She emerged only temporarily, however, and it is probable that her defeat occurred ultimately for the same reasons everywhere: the economic depression. In America, the New Deal did not rely on the scapegoating of minority groups and on an ideology of female inferiority and male dominance to achieve its economic and political goals. In Germany, Adolf Hitler and his new order reestablished the old images of masculinity and femininity—with a vengeance.

Women's role in Nazi Germany was narrowed to emphasize the breeding of Aryan men and women for the glory of the Third Reich. Sex typing and segregation were extreme—in school, in recreation, and in the family. In labor camps and in youth organizations, girls were taught the age-old peasant virtues and values—obedience, hard work, service to males, and, now, service to the state.

The ideal male role also contained an exaggeration of traditional conceptions, bordering on the caricature. Male aggression was glorified in the name of nationalism and war. Male friendship was so greatly romanticized that homosexuality became far more manifest than before. Women were stigmatized as genetically inferior and potentially destructive—a usual feature of societies characterized by extreme sex typing.

World War II and the need for female workers in the war economy tempered the situation somewhat, once again. And the labor shortages and the surplus of women in the two Germanies since 1949 have promoted a breakdown in sex typing, at least within the middle occupational levels. West Germany today is far more industrialized that East Germany. But socialist ideology in the German Democratic Republic has resulted in a greater decline in sex typing in that country. A larger percentage of women in East Germany are employed in the industrial economy, and higher proportions are enrolled in institutions of higher learning (35).

Religious ideologies have also mediated the effects of industrialization on the roles and identities of men and women in various countries. In Protestant countries women have accepted and acted upon the modern, urban values more rapidly than in Catholic countries. It is difficult to separate the effect of the Protestant religion as an independent factor in promoting change, however, since Protestant countries are also more industrialized.

Where socialist governments have made systematic attempts to abolish formal religion, the changes in the roles of men and women have been most rapid and most dramatic, particularly among the young in urban areas and regardless of the strength of preexisting religious and philosophical orientations. But tradition lingers on, everywhere in the self- conceptions, personalities, hopes, and expectations of men and women—despite differing historical circumstances and political and economic conditions. Even in the United States, traditional conceptions of the ideal behavior and personality traits of men and women are still most prevalent in all segments of the population. Included here are most college students, who, by virtue of age and education, would be expected to be least traditional in this respect (36).

We can now understand better the historical trend in the typical identities of men and women, as well as the variations that persist today in major areas of the world. Where science and technology are at similar stages of development, the strength of preexisting traditional values accounts for many of the differences that exist.

Such values are incorporated into the roles that women and men learn. These different role conceptions result in typically different self conceptions and identities. As values change—in the direction of greater individualism, equalitarianism, tolerance, rationalism, and secularism—ideals of masculinity and femininity change, roles change, and identities change, slowly but inevitably.

The underlying force is technological development and the increases in economic and educational opportunities that this process brings. But national differences in the strength of traditional values and in the degree of sex typing hasten or slow the effects of technological development.

A further look at one country, the United States, illustrates clearly the relative weight of technology and values in changing the relationships and the typical identities of the sexes. The United States is not only the most technologically developed nation in the world, it is also the most heterogeneous. The emphasis on the traditional values varies in the many subcultures of class, race, national origin, and age. Sex role conceptions and self conceptions also vary, typically, in these several social universes. The process of change in the relationships and identities of the sexes can be seen, simultaneously, in its many varieties and in its major directions in the United States.

Finally, there is a practical reason for focusing on America. The woman's movement has been relatively strong in the United States, and recently social scientists have been very busy providing more knowledge about how and why the sexes differ in their self images and in their behavior.

What are the typical differences in personality, role conceptions, status, and behavior that distinguish boys and girls and men and women in various segments of American society? How can we explain the similarities and differences that exist? To what extent are they unique? And to what extent are they typical of industrialized nations around the world?

5 | Sexual Identity in America

In all societies, even those in which sex typing is not extreme, a person's basic status is that of male or female, and this basic status determines what other statuses the person can or cannot have.

Since sexual status results in the learning of sex-typed personality traits and behavior and a sex-typed self image or identity, gender also affects the performance of all roles people play (1). The status of student is equally open to girls and boys, at least at the levels below graduate and professional school. But females and males play out the role of student somewhat differently, typically, as a result of their earlier sex-typed learning experiences.

Women college students are less apt to cut classes. They are less likely to participate in controversial classroom discussions. They write longer papers and exams, usually. They have fewer reading problems, their handwriting is more legible, and their grammar and spelling are more accurate. They sit more quietly, take more notes, and are less likely to earn C's than male students (2). Young girls in American society are taught to compete and to value achievement, at least at the lower grade levels, and especially in the middle class. In addition, they are typically expected to be more obedient and conforming than their male peers. And this expectation affects their performance as students, as it affects all other roles that they play.

Males and females tend to experience different conflicts about their roles, or they experience the same conflicts, but with very different degrees of intensity, varying according to the stage in the life cycle and according to class and ethnic (national) origin. For example, black male adolescents and white middle-aged females have different conflicts about their roles and their identities.

Sex typing exists in all segments of American society, although it varies somewhat in degree within the different classes and ethnic groups. Conceptions of the ideal female or male are still quite widely held, however, despite the rise of the women's movement, changing economic and political conditions, and the continued spread of modern values, such as individualism and equalitarianism.

Research on sex roles by anthropologists and sociologists has focused on culturally and subculturally defined conceptions of masculinity and femininity, as these have varied in place and time. Such conceptions are learned by most people, beginning at birth, within the family, and they are usually reinforced throughout the society and throughout the life cycle. These conceptions determine the basic identity or self image that is typical of men and women in a specific society at any given time.

The concept of sex role is, in a sense, a misnomer. It does not refer to something that can be observed and measured as a distinct and separate entity. A person never relates to another only as a male or as a female, but as father to son, mother to daughter, or employee to employer. Gender, the background status underlying the other statuses that people have, varies in importance depending on these other statuses. Gender is very prominent in family roles; it should not be prominent, although it often is, in the performance of occupational roles. When students make comments about the sexiness of a female teacher, they are responding primarily to her status as female. When patients in a hospital are startled to learn that the man in white who is attending them is a nurse, they are responding to his status as a male.

The learning of sex-typed roles that embody culturally defined conceptions of masculinity and femininity results in typically different personality traits for males and females. Psychologists have studied the development and existence of differences in behavior, thought, and emotion in male and female children and adults. Insofar as these differences are typical, they tend to be largely a product of common sex-typed learning experiences based on differing role expectations for males and females.

Personality and identity are more than a product of role playing, however. Many men and women do not conform to the typical, for a variety of reasons. Every individual who is not an identical twin is constitutionally unique, and no two individuals grow up in totally similar environments. When I speak about the typical, I am referring to the statistically most frequent. This is generalizing, not stereotyping. Stereotypes are either completely false or they are exaggerated statements or beliefs about a particular group of people. They are exaggerated if what is true of a *small* number of these people is applied indiscriminately to *all* members of the group. In speaking of typical differences in the personalities of males and females, I am describing what is true of *most* (but by no means all) males and females in contemporary American society, and my descriptions are based on research, not on preconception or prejudice.

Much of the research on sex differences in identity, personality, and behavior, has been conducted on infants, children, and young adults. But many of the typical sex differences that I describe here diminish, disappear, or become reversed in later life cycle stages of most men and women. It is important to remember this, also, when reading reviews of research findings on sex differences. Statistically, typical differences appear on various psychological tests, particularly of young people. To ignore these differences because they sometimes seem to reflect unfavorably on either of the sexes is to avoid the problem. We need to understand and explain sex differences, thereby putting ourselves in a better position to eliminate those that increase human suffering unnecessarily.

MALE AND FEMALE PERSONALITY DIFFERENCES.

Studies of sex-typed personality traits of infants, children, and adults in the United States have employed a large variety of methods. The survey research questionnaire has been the most common tool for determining typical differences in motivation, thought, and behavior in males and females. Survey research can reach many people, rather quickly. However, the information obtained tends to be rather fragmented and superficial.

A number of other techniques, used on smaller populations, have provided deeper kinds of information about sex-typed differences in personality. Projective instruments—Rorschach tests and Thematic Apperception Tests—have been used to determine unconscious fantasies, impulses, and motives that are not revealed on attitude questionnaires. Since most people learn and tend to accept culturally defined conceptions of masculinity and femininity, they are apt to deny or fail to recognize impulses or traits that are prescribed for the opposite sex.

Projective tests can supply information that is less distorted by mechanisms of defense, demonstrating how effective sex role learning has actually been, regardless of superficial appearances. Unfortunately, this type of research is very time-consuming and very costly, and since only small populations can be studied, there is always a question about whether the results of projective studies are typical or representative of large numbers of people.

Recently attempts have been made to combine the advantages of the survey questionnaire and projective test types of studies. It has been learned that people are more likely to reveal their deeper or less acceptable feelings and impulses when they are asked to comment on a statement about others, instead of responding to a direct question about themselves. Investigators are using these more sophisticated approaches with growing frequency. Questionnaires are more apt to include projective type questions, particularly in sensitive areas, to which people might be likely to respond defensively. If researchers are interested in finding out how many women would like to have an extramarital affair, for example, their result will be more accurate if they ask women to agree or disagree with the statement: "Most women would like to have an extramarital affair" than if they ask "Would you like to have an affair?" Another way of increasing the accuracy of the responses obtained on questions about marital happiness would be to ask "Would you make the same choice again, if you had it to do over again?" rather than, "How happily married are you?"

Observational studies of males and females in natural settings —in schools, at work, or at home—have also served to provide information on sex differences. The use of video tape and tape recorders, which help correct for the biases and possible prejudices of investigators, has improved tremendously the accuracy of observational studies of sex-typed behavior. The data are there. No one can argue with the contents of a tape or a film— anyone can hear or see the results. It becomes less possible to selectively perceive or report sex-typed differences if more objective means of recording such differences are used.

Experimental studies have been another very important source of information on typical differences in the personalities of females and males. In this type of work, the effects of certain conditions, or stimuli, are measured in a carefully controlled environment—the differential response of men and women to propaganda, for example, or to the same artificially created frustrating conditions. A major problem is the impossibility of duplicating the extremely complex social environments of human beings in the laboratory. We cannot know that the responses we observe in the laboratory would occur under natural circumstances. We cannot predict, for example, that an individual who

behaves very aggressively in a laboratory experiment will behave very aggressively elsewhere.

Despite the problems in the several approaches and techniques that have been used to study sex differences in
personality, social scientists have accumulated a large amount of
information on the topic in recent years. And despite much
overlapping and many exceptions, the results of most studies reveal widespread and continuing typical differences in the personalities of female and male infants, children, and young
adults.

Personality Differences. On various psychological tests and in
many experimental and observational studies, more males than
females have been physically aggressive—and they have felt less
guilt and anxiety about their aggressions when expressing them.
Larger percentages of females have displayed dependent attitudes and behavior and have exhibited the following traits or
behavior patterns: strong concern with popularity, seeking help
and approval from peers and authority figures, conformity to
rules and ready acceptance of authority, expression of socially
acceptable attitudes, conservative approach to taking risks, and
higher susceptibility to propaganda (3).

In other psychological studies, larger percentages of females
have openly displayed sympathy, affection, and helpfulness,
have confided readily in others, and have known intimate de-
tails about others. More females have better verbal skills—they
learn to speak sooner, articulate more clearly, and use longer
sentences, better grammar, and more correct spelling. Girls are
also more likely to receive better grades in elementary school
and in high school and to do equally well on all subjects. A
larger percentage of males do well in courses that interest them
and poorly in subjects they dislike.

In doll play, on drawing tests, and on projective tests, more girls than boys make people responses. On tests of memory, more girls have better memories for names and faces. On tests of rote memory, however—on the digit span test of the Wechsler Intelligence Scale for children—no significant sex differences have been reported.

Larger percentages of males in various studies have tested out as independent—self sufficient, self directing, and self controlling. In small group studies, males typically have taken on the role of leader; females typically have played mediating or tension-breaking roles.

There are no significant differences in the performances of males and females on tests of adult intelligence, but since items on intelligence tests are standardized to eliminate sex differences, this is not surprising. Other differences that appear on tests of intellectual functioning seem to be clearly related to sex-typed learning experiences. More females than males seem to have difficulty expressing intellectual as well as emotional independence. At least this has been the argument used to explain typical differences that have been found between males and females in "breaking set" on certain psychological tests. Such differences have shown up on embedded figures tests (pick out the barely visible figures from the background), the rod and frame test (place the rod upright within a skewed frame), and spatial relationship tests (match widely separated forms or structures). Fewer females than males have performed well on these tests.

With many of these results, and with most other sex differences that have been observed in psychological tests, however, it is important to note that typical differences do not appear, or are reversed, on tests of very young children. This is also true of tests of abilities, such as mathematical reasoning or manual dexterity. And many of the differences that have been reported, diminish in later stages of the life cycle. Clearly, learned, sex-typed roles strongly affect temperament and abilities as children age. And as roles change, in old age, so does personality.

Achievement Motivation. The need for achievement is a need to excel according to some standard of accomplishment—wealth, political power, popularity, gourmet cooking, or creative home furnishing. In psychological tests of achievement motivation, accomplishment has usually been defined in terms of career goals or other rewards that are sex typed for males. In the United States, therefore, early studies of achievement motivation and competition were done on males (4). Not enough females could be aroused to compete for the goals as defined in experimental situations by psychologists—goals such as a chance for high level employment in government or industry.

In thinking about the research on achievement motivation, it is important to remember that many women have a very strong need to compete and to achieve, but this need is channeled into the traditional goals and rewards that are more readily available to females. Their standards of excellence and their strivings are directed toward achieving success in marriage, childrearing, homemaking, and volunteer and community activities.

Thus we have seen why studies measuring competitive drives toward career goals favor males, statistically. More females opt for sociability and popularity instead of career achievement. First of all, as females they have the option—and, often, the encouragement—to do so. But also, being well-liked and being very successful do not go together. Not everybody loves a winner; winners are not loved by losers. And those who compete successfully have less time for friends.

In a now classic study performed in 1965, at a large urban university, it was found that many women college students have a far greater need to avoid success than their fellow male students (5). These women had high levels of achievement motivation, but they feared social rejection, loss of femininity, and mental breakdown as a consequence of outstanding achievement. Competition was more often stressful for them than for male students, especially when they were tested in mixed-sex groups.

This study has been repeated a number of times on other groups, with very interesting results. Black women, particularly from the working class, do not show this fear of success (6). In their subculture, competence, independence, and resourcefulness are not defined as unfeminine. Black college women of middle class origin, however, are closer to the white pattern. Black males score as high as white females on the fear of success.

A repetition of the original study at the same college campus revealed a striking change, however (7). Six years later, in 1971, a large percentage of women still tested out as having a need to avoid success. An almost equally high percentage of males showed the same response, but for different reasons. The male students who needed to avoid success did not fear unpopularity or loss of their sexual identity. They very likely were displaying the effects of the youth counterculture, which was strong on the subject campus. Antimaterialism is a central feature of the counterculture. The "hang loose" fun ethic supplants the "up tight" work ethic and the singleminded pursuit of wealth and success (8). Very strong achievement drives, indulged in at the expense of love and friendship, are rejected by counterculture members. It is very hard to love your sisters and your brothers if their A's mean your B. This difficulty reflects a basic conflict in American culture, incidentally—a culture that emphasizes individualism and excellence and, at the same time, gregariousness and equalitarianism.

Since conflict about achievement in careers tends to be more frequent in women, what information do we have about women who manage to overcome this conflict? What is true about the family backgrounds, personalities, and life experiences of women who succeed—especially in professional and administrative occupations that are sex-typed for males?

Most earlier studies of successful women emphasized negative aspects in their social relationships (with their mothers, in particular). Women who became doctors, lawyers, and scientists were found to be unusually independent. This trait was traced to a lack, stemming from "maternal hostility" and rejection, of a close relationship with the subjects' mothers (9). Career women were described as having identified with their fathers, and particularly with paternal achievement values. Investigators also focused on the frustrations, dissatisfactions, and identity confusions of successful women, and on the parental conflicts in their childhood homes that had led to a rejection of the traditional feminine role (10).

More recently, and very likely in response to the women's movement, successful women, particularly those in male-dominated professions, are receiving different treatment in the social scientific literature. The emphasis now is on the lack of overprotection or "smother love" in the mother–daughter relationship, rather than on maternal rejection (11). Career women are now described in terms of their abilities in specific areas—math or science, for example. In the past, they were described as having "masculine interests." The career-oriented daughter, in more recent studies, has been found to identify with her mother as well as with her father, especially when the mother herself works or has a career (12).

The new and seemingly contradictory studies, pointing to positive elements in the personalities and life experiences of career-oriented women, are not contradictory at all. They reflect the different times in which the studies were conducted and the changing social context in American society today. Far more mothers, of all ages and all classes, are working now than ever before. These women serve as models for their daughters and, at the same time, they are less available to overprotect their offspring. The phenomenon of "momism" occurs when a woman whose strong career drives are blocked, turns mothering into a career. Working mothers do not usually have the time, energy, or need to overprotect or overinvest in their children.

Children identify strongly with models who are perceived as warm and nurturing. They identify with people who are viewed as having desired traits or resources—power, love, or competence in areas that the child feels are important (13). With the rising status and changing roles of women, aspiring daughters are more likely to identify with their mothers as well as with their fathers. And if their mothers have personality traits, such as self-reliance and assertiveness, that are usually sex-typed for the opposite sex, daughters, too, will acquire these traits.

Origins and Continuities. The constantly multiplying studies of male and female personality differences point to the more frequent occurrence of traits of passivity, dependence, and conformity in females in American society. Good little boys are sissies; good little girls are feminine. However, sex-typed expectations on the part of families, teachers, and friends are far more important than anatomy, hormones, and chromosomes in establishing and promoting these sex differences in personality.

Studies of similarities and differences in the intellectual and emotional functioning of black and white males and females support the foregoing argument. Black males and white females are more conforming; black females and white males are more independent and resourceful (14). These results reflect similarities in social expectations and in the availability of objective opportunities. Black males and white females do not have like anatomical, chromosomal, or hormonal constitutions. They do, however, experience similar disabilities in their attempts to fulfill their achievement needs.

Some differences in typical male and female personality traits appear within the first year of life. In one study, mother–child contact and behavior was observed in the home when infants were three weeks old and then again when they were three months old (15). Male infants cried more, slept less, and were more active when awake. Mothers responded by holding, rocking, burping, looking at, and talking to their male infants more than to their female infants. The author explains the more frequent contact between the mothers and their male children as a response to the greater wakefulness, activity, and irritability of the little boys. The "state" affects the quantity and the quality of the mother's response. At the same time, mothers during both observational periods were more apt to imitate and reinforce the random sounds made by their female infants.

It has been argued that the typical differences in the mood states and behavior of male and female infants is genetic in origin; I feel, however, that maternal expectations are also very important in eliciting the greater activity and irritability of male infants. Boys, by cultural definition, are not expected to be calm and good and passive. These expectations begin to operate, very subtly, and very effectively, at the moment of birth. And infants respond to these expectations. Certainly the greater tendency of mothers to imitate and react to the random sounds produced by their female infants may be due to an expectation that female infants will be more verbal, and sooner, than male infants. Such unconscious expectations are difficult to tap, but they should be investigated further.

By the time infants are six months old, and even more by the time they are a year old, typical sex-typed behavior and personality traits are obvious and easily observed (16). At these ages, female infants are touched, held, caressed, kissed, smiled at, and talked to more frequently by their mothers. Male infants at the age of one year tend to respond to frustration by fighting; girls of the same age are more likely to cry helplessly. Year-old boys more frequently venture farther away from their mothers, stay away longer, look at their mothers less, and play more vigorously with toys.

The sex-typed norms for male and female behavior are learned very early. Starting in infancy, most boys are taught to be independent, to explore, and to master the world. Most girls are taught to be conforming and dependent. Both sexes experience typical, but different, emotional repressions. For many males, the necessity to curb gentleness, affection, sentiment, and anxiety results in the inexpressive male—of the cowboy or playboy variety (17). The cowboy type, as portrayed by John Wayne (and by Gary Cooper, on occasion), is strong, silent, two-fisted, tough, and 100 per cent American. He loves his woman, but he shows more affection to his horse, and he loves duty even more.

In modern times the cowboy has evolved into the playboy type—cool, resourceful, manipulative, detached, and exploitative. The playboy does not love his women (notice the plural). He shows no affection toward man, woman, or beast. He is not committed to work, marriage, or any other routine responsibility. The playboy of the 1970s is even more inexpressive than his nineteenth century counterpart. He has no feelings to suppress.

Females are usually required to repress aggression, with consequences that have long been celebrated in literature, theology, and philosophy. Recently the damage done to both sexes by this kind of repression has become more recognized, at least in the social scientific literature (18). The very traditional woman is more apt to develop gynecological and obstetrical disorders, less apt to enjoy sex, and more apt to have postpartum and postmenopausal depressions. In modern societies, she is likely to be a burden to herself, to her husband, and to her children.

Role Conflict. Conflict in the acting out of a role is experienced as frustration, arising from many sources—unfulfilled expectations, contradictory or impossible demands of the role, the incompatible demands of several roles, or a lack of adequate or appropriate resources (physical, intellectual, emotional, or economic) for performing the role. Individuals who experience role conflict often feel torn in opposite directions, or they feel inadequate or unsuited to performing a role.

Many role conflicts are built into roles—by definition. Parents must love their children, but they must also discipline their children. These are often contradictory responses, however, since disciplining may be done in anger and it is difficult to feel loving when one is angry.

Males and females tend to have different role conflicts or, typically, they experience the same conflicts with differing degrees of intensity. Authoritarian fathers, for example, are more apt to experience the conflict between the need to discipline and the need to love and be loved by children. Most males are required to be independent; yet in modern societies, they are dependent for ever-lengthening periods of time during adolescence and old age. This is probably a more frequent source of conflict for men than for women, whose (current) concept of femininity is not typically threatened by dependency.

Women who play the dual role may experience strong conflicts over the incompatible demands of their familial and economic roles. Time and energy are limited, but demands of employers, family, and friends tend to be unlimited, particularly in modern times, when role expectations become ambiguous (19). Men may experience this kind of conflict also, expecially if they define their family role to include active participation in child-rearing and homemaking.

The traditional sex-typed personality traits are poorly suited to the demands of modern life and modern social relationships. This, too, typically, results in somewhat different conflicts for men and women. The inexpressive male may find it difficult to meet contemporary standards in husband–wife and parent–child relationships—standards that require psychological intimacy and mutual emotional support (20). On the other hand, women who grow up sheltered, protected, and dependent are ill-equipped to make many decisions that they must make, by default, in modern societies. The husband may not be available to act as the ultimate authority. He may be away at work or simply not interested in the day-to-day decision-making crises that are common in rapidly changing societies.

Females, particularly those in the middle class, are expected to compete equally and aggressively with males in school, expecially at the lower levels. In adulthood, however, they are also expected to be receptive, nurturing, and dependent in their relationships with men. This requires a rather delicate compromise on the part of women who have learned their achievement lessons well.

The conflict between the simultaneous needs to compete and to be well liked appears to be greater for women—particularly those who have strong achievement drives. Individuals who are autonomous and less dependent on others for approval or disapproval can step on toes with less guilt and anxiety.

The mental shutdown that many adult women experience does not prepare them to fulfill the companionship role that is expected of them in the middle and upper classes, particularly in the later stages of the life cycle. The uneven psychological growth rates of men and women, expecially when the husband is highly educated and ambitious, probably constitute a major reason for the current epidemic of divorces, after ten or twenty years of marriage, in the upper middle class.

The young, bright woman drops out of college to support her husband through professional or graduate school. She then proceeds to have children. And she never manages to complete her education. Her professional or managerial husband, meanwhile, continues to expand his interests, knowledge, and horizons. In middle age, when the children begin to depart, the discrepancies in psychological growth between husband and wife may become a problem, given the need for companionship and sharing of interests in modern nuclear families, which are increasingly turned in on themselves.

Because of sex-typed learning experiences, the need for security tends to be stronger in most women than the need for challenge. And this need is less apt to be gratified, given the uncertain and unpredictable nature of modern life (21). As extended family relationships and friendship networks break down in mobile societies, the stronger need for sociability that characterizes many women is also more likely to be a source of frustration to them than to men. Women who do not work and who are not otherwise actively involved in nonfamily activities are most likely to experience the loneliness and the disconnectedness promoted by individualistic values and geographic and social mobility.

Since women's roles are changing more rapidly than men's in

modern or modernizing societies, it is women who bear the major burdens and frustrations of working out new relationships with men, other women, and children. Women are more likely to make new demands; men are more likely to deny them. A lack of mutuality in expectations becomes a source of conflict for both sexes—but the initiators of change are more vulnerable.

Urban middle class males around the world increasingly want educated, interesting wives as companions. But highly educated women with career goals may be a threat to the norm of male intellectual superiority. In the working class, the threat of the working wife centers on the possible infringement on the male's role as economic provider.

Studies of college men and women at elite colleges in the United States, particularly the pioneering research by Mirra Komarovsky, point to a change in sex-typed expectations and conflicts over the past thirty years (22). In the early 1940s bright college women often played dumb to attract men and to sustain the image of femininity. In the early 1970s college women were less apt to conceal their talents, and college males claimed that they preferred strong, competent, independent, and resourceful women. But male intellectual superiority was still regarded as important in specific relationships by both sexes (23). Moreover, despite the change in attitude toward female intellectuality and competence, at least on the part of males at elite colleges, these men nevertheless expected the wives they would one day have to stay at home full-time and play the traditional role—at least while the children were very young.

The expectation that very competent wives will interrupt their careers for motherhood is not in itself a potential major source of conflict between the sexes, since a majority of career-oriented middle class high school and college women want and expect to stay at home full-time while their children are young (24). This attitude may be less a matter of strong maternal sentiment and more a reaction to the absence of good alternatives, however. Good nursery and day care facilities are not available on a large scale. Members of the extended family are also unavailable, particularly in the mobile middle class. And highly educated husbands are often too preoccupied with their own career obligations to provide much help.

The major conflict in the situation just outlined arises from the incompatibility of the personality traits of highly educated, career-oriented women and the demands of the full-time, traditional homemaking and childrearing role. Women who have experienced freedom and independence in pursuit of educational and occupational opportunities are poorly prepared for the abrupt curtailment of both, which occurs with the birth of a child. A solution is not imminent in America, and the problem will grow worse as more and more women from the working class as well as the middle class, go on to higher education. The percentage of women entering college has been rising slowly but steadily in recent years. (Women comprised almost half the freshmen class in colleges in the United States in 1972.) And there is no reason to assume that this trend will not continue, whatever the fate of the women's movement.

The optimistic expectation that it will all work out if educated women interrupt their careers during the early years of childrearing does not seem to be a very realistic one. The woman who is in a rapidly changing field may not be able to catch up when she returns to work or school. Besides, people are often unable to anticipate accurately how they will feel when they enter a new stage in the life cycle. We have very few studies of what actually happens when women with strong achievement needs interrupt or give up careers to raise children. The studies that are available indicate that such women have lower self-esteem and experience higher levels of frustration, dissatisfaction, and depression than women who do not interrupt their careers (25).

The career versus motherhood problem would be more severe when the women involved have gone on to complete their training and education before starting a family. This, moreover, appears to be a pattern that is becoming more frequent among younger women professionals. With each additional year of training or work in the field, commitment to the career increases, and the shift to full-time mothering and homemaking, even temporarily, would be correspondingly harder to make.

Another problem that may arise in two-career families stems from the tendency for highly motivated females to be more disciplined in the pursuit of academic goals. They may achieve more recognition than their husbands, if they are not too incapacitated by family obligations. Particularly when the husband and wife are in the same professional field, the threat to the husband may be serious, given the persistence of the norm of male superiority. The possibility of divorce looms larger then. The divorce rate of women with graduate degrees is higher than the rate that is typical for middle class women (26).

LIFE CYCLE SEX DIFFERENCES. The tendency for sex typing to become less extreme as individuals age, is probably the most striking feature that emerges from studies of typical changes in values, personality traits, and behavior of human beings, from infancy to old age (27). Men become less aggressive and less achievement-oriented, and more affectionate, gentle and more sentimental. The grandfather often can express more love and warmth to his grandchildren than he was able to express toward his own children. The older woman, whose children are grown, becomes less self-sacrificing, more independent, assertive, and egocentric (28).

In studies of the family life cycle, men and women have the most equalitarian relationships within the early years of marriage, before the children are born. With the birth of a child, and increasingly with each successive child that is born, the authority of mothers declines and roles tend to shift toward more traditional patterns. This pattern varies, of course, according to class, level of education of the marital partners, and whether the mother is employed.

Given the lengthened life span in highly industrial societies, the far greater tendency for women to be gainfully employed, and the tendency for males to marry women who are younger than they are, a sex role reversal in the later stages of married life is becoming more frequent in American society. Retired men, married to younger women who are still employed, tend to take over many homemaking obligations. They prepare breakfast for their working wives, do the laundry and marketing, and generally assume greater responsibility for household operations (29). The authority of the female in this situation is quite high. Indeed, she is often dominant in the relationship, and since power is related to economic resources, this is understandable. Women are also more likely to have the resource of physical health to back up their authority during this stage in the family life cycle.

Reports of the marital satisfaction of women, in the middle class particularly, tend to follow this same pattern. Many middle class women report a decline in marital happiness during the childrearing period, followed by a rise after the children have grown and left home (30). Men do not experience this pattern, very likely because childrearing is not a direct burden for them. Incidentally, men also express higher marital satisfaction generally. Jessie Bernard has synthesized a great deal of research data on this topic (31). She feels that the isolation of the unemployed housewife is a major source of the stress women experience in contemporary marriages. Husbands, who have other outlets, especially at work, are apt to be less involved in the marital relationship as a primary or only source of emotional gratification.

During all stages of the life cycle, culturally defined norms regulate behavior to some extent. Hence the admonition: "Act your age!" Most people are substantially agreed about the behavior that is appropriate for various stages of the life cycle. This consensus is implicit in statements such as "She is pretty liberal for someone her age."

Young people are far less rigid about acting their age, however. Twenty-year-olds, asked whether they think it is right for seventeen-year-olds to marry, are likely to reply "I suppose it would be all right if the boy got a good job, and if they loved each other. Why not? It isn't age that's the important thing." Forty-five-year-old people, in contrast, are likely to respond: "At that age, they'd be foolish. Neither of them is settled enough. A boy on his own, at seventeen, couldn't support a wife, and he certainly couldn't support children (32).

As a rule, the young will also be much more venturesome about adopting patterns of dress, speech, and behavior that are defined as appropriate for other age groups. The recent vogue among many female adolescents of dressing in infant-style clothing is an example. Sixty-five-year-old women are not likely to wear mini skirts, although this usage varies by class. Upper class women are more daring. Staying young-looking is vitally important to them in their companion role.

Males, generally, are less restricted by age norms than are females, since sex-typed requirements to conform are usually more pressing on the female sex. The pressures to marry and bear children within a particular age range are stronger for females than for males. The speech and dress of the youth counterculture has been adopted more readily by middle-aged males than by middle-aged females. Many middle-aged males, especially in the middle class, are wearing their hair longer; not many women in this age group have discarded lipstick and bras. Males are more apt to marry much younger women. Older women rarely marry much younger men, at least not in the United States. In old age, however, both sexes tend to become more conservative about age-appropriate behavior.

Aging is a biological process, but perception of where a person is in the life cycle tends to be less a matter of biological age than a reflection of changes in family life or in work histories. For women, motherhood most often defines full adult status; and the departure of the youngest child from home usually coincides with the feeling of being middle-aged. Men tend to define themselves as adults, middle-aged, or old in terms of their occupational status. The first full-time job symbolizes adulthood. The final promotion defines middle-age for those who have the possibility of promotion within bureaucratic hierarchies. Sometimes being passed over for promotion by younger employees has the same result. Men see old age as signified by retirement—compulsory or voluntary. For men, also, abrupt changes in physical health (e.g., the development of a chronic illness) often precipitate the feeling of having shifted into the status of middle or old age.

The strains, conflicts, and frustrations characteristic of the various stages of the life cycle also differ, typically, for women and men. In modern societies, adolescents of both sexes are confronted with the problems of working out their adult identities and coping with their heightened sexual drives. Young women who do not plan careers (and the majority of female adolescents do not) have no problem about making a choice in this area. They do not have to ask "What will I be when I grow up?" They will be wives and mothers. They will work if their husbands do not earn an adequate income, if they are unmarried, divorced, or deserted, or if they choose to work. And if they work, they will be very likely to take undemanding, routine jobs, requiring little commitment and affecting identity only minimally and incidentally.

Males, on the other hand, and particularly in the middle class, do have alternative paths available, and the decision about what they will be when they grow up becomes more and more difficult as possibilities multiply and competititon increases. But unlike many women, males do not have the choice of staying out of the labor market altogether.

The need to be independent and autonomous is still a trait

that is sex-typed for males rather than for females in American society; thus, given the longer years of economic dependency of modern adolescents, fulfilling this need is also a more frequent problem for males. To be dependent may be frustrating to many young women also, but it does not usually threaten their conception of themselves as feminine. More often, young women face the necessity of coping with strong achievement motivation and competitiveness. The problem of economic dependency, for both sexes, is very strong in countries like the United States, where the government does not directly assume the financial burden of educating and supporting students in colleges and professional schools.

The strain of establishing friendships and love relationships is probably more frequent for female adolescents, given their greater dependency, preoccupation with popularity, and investment in the marital relationship, at least at the present time. Dating and free choice of marital partners opens up a universe of possibilities in modern societies, simultaneously exposing participants in the dating game to unprecedented insecurities and competition. In a society in which physical attractiveness in women is still more highly valued than competence or intelligence, the attractive female will be at a distinct advantage. She is more likely to marry up in the social scale, and she is more likely to marry a man who will be successful (33).

Coping with the heightened sexual drives of adolescence is a problem for both sexes in restrictive societies, but many young women in contemporary America are especially subject to the conflicts stemming from more severe childhood sexual repressions and from ignorance about the biology of sex and about contraception. A number of studies indicate that sexual problems trouble many women in America (34). Even women who achieve orgasm are usually unable to do so in a majority of their sexual encounters. And this problem is reported, despite the rapid increase in premarital sexual activity since the mid-1960s, particularly among middle class college women (35).

With the spread of the fun ethic and counterculture values, the discrepancy between attitudes and behavior in this area seems to have declined somewhat. In the past, sexual activity on the part of young, unmarried women often was seen by them as being contradictory to their attitudes, which placed a high value on virginity. Now fewer women feel they have gone "too far" (36).

Evidence is beginning to accumulate that indicates the re-emergence of the "new woman," among young, middle class, college-educated females. This type of woman, sexually and psychologically liberated, first made her appearance in this country on a relatively large scale in the 1920s. She went under ground, thereafter, and stayed there, for the most part, until the mid-1960s.

In a recent study, a majority of college women who were involved in the living-together relationship characterized themselves as independent, assertive, and outgoing (37). They were no less likely to characterize themselves in this way than the college males in the study who were unmarried and cohabiting with a member of the opposite sex. More traditional women, however, who would not engage in a living-together relationship under any circumstances, were far more apt to characterize themselves as dependent, shy, and unassertive.

The new woman—educated, independent, assertive, and increasingly like males in self image, attitude, and behavior—was reared in a permissive home, where sex typing was not extreme. Although she is hardly typical in American society today, she is very likely a harbinger of the change to come.

As mentioned earlier, the second principal source of difficulties and conflict in the attempts of many young women to cope with the heightened sexual drives of adolescence stems from ignorance about the sexual act and about contraceptive techniques. This problem does not seem to be easing much, although the fear of pregnancy and illegitimacy may be lessened when legal abortion becomes readily available to all. But awareness that an abortion can be obtained, if necessary, is a rather drastic means of allaying anxiety about pregnancy. Sex education and reliable information on preventive contraceptive techniques are still unavailable to a majority of young women in America. Many high school students, for example, believe that the safest time to engage in intercourse without contraception is during the middle of the menstrual cycle (38). The problems stemming from such ignorance are more severe for working class high school girls, since they are somewhat more likely than middle class girls to engage in sexual intercourse during the high school years; moreover, they are even less likely than middle class girls to be correctly informed about contraception and the biology of reproduction and the sexual act.

Middle age is another time in the life cycle when men and women experience typically different conflicts and stresses. The experience of loss is typical for both sexes in middle age: the deaths of aged parents and of contemporary friends, the departure of grown children, and the loss of energy and good health.

The loss of grown children who move away and establish their own autonomous households is likely to be more painful for women, especially those who have felt more committed to their children than to their husbands. Other women, particularly in the middle class, who have not overinvested in their children, will not feel the loss as sharply. Women who have played the partner role, in fact, may feel more joy than sorrow at the maturity of their children. They will feel less guilt about their work activities and will feel freer to pursue them.

In middle age an individual's time perspective shifts from time elapsed since birth to time left to live. This change, which can be traumatic, tends to have its significance for different reasons in men and in women. Those who are dissatisfied are more apt to engage in a life review. Typically, dissatisfactions center on the family for women and on failures in job achievement for men. Women may be faced with disappointment in their children, particularly if they expect too much (and traditional women often do). The payoff from grateful children never comes. And many men face the realization that childhood dreams of fame and fortune, or even of mild success, will never be realized.

It is a tragedy of modern existence that the aging men and women who have played out the traditional roles with the strongest commitment are the ones who will experience the greatest stress when their sex-typed personality traits and behavior are no longer appropriate to their changing status in life. For women in middle age, such stress is typically triggered when family obligations and preoccupations decline. For men, old age is the big inconsistency. And those who are hardest hit are those who have been most invested in work and in the success ethic (39).

Men who end up in mental hospitals after retirement are very likely to be those who continue to feel that popularity can be achieved only by superior power and wealth. They retain an orientation toward acquiring money and other material rewards that they can no longer have. They continue to fight aggressively against the frustrations of old age. They define loss as a personal shortcoming. They compete and strive, but in a vacuum, and life loses all meaning and purpose.

I anticipate that this gloomy prospect will lighten for younger generations, and particularly for the women and men who have grown up with the experience of less extreme sex typing and more flexible sexual identities.

CLASS DIFFERENCES. Class is a loaded concept that evokes disapproval from many Americans, who prefer to use terms such as interest or income groups, socioeconomic status, or social inequality. This distaste for the concept of class stems from the equalitarian ideology in the United States and the association of class analysis with Marxian socialist theory. Class exists, however, and it cannot be defined away. It is an objective fact based on observable, measurable differences between people in modern societies. People who are members of a particular class have similar amounts of prestige, power, and wealth relative to other people in the society. They are ranked in categories above and below one another, and they tend to associate and marry other individuals from the same class. Although people may not be aware of where they belong in the class structure, classes exist, nonetheless.

The factors that determine class vary in different societies. Ancestry is very important in agricultural societies. In technologically developed societies, personal qualities—intelligence, resourcefulness, ambition—as these affect occupational achievement, acquire great significance.

Occupation is the most accurate indicator of class. When sociologists are limited by time and money in their attempts to describe the class structure of a community, they determine the occupational structure of that community. Occupation is very closely related to educational level and income, and these factors are, in turn, very closely related to the values, attitudes, role conceptions, childrearing practices, and typical sexual identities of children, adolescents, adults, and old people.

There is much blurring and overlapping in the class structure of the United States. However, if we divide the population into three major classes (upper, middle, and working), we find typical differences in life styles and life chances among people. These distinctions affect relationships between the sexes in predictable ways, for large numbers of people, and despite individual variability.

The key to the similarity in sexual identities in the major classes is the tendency of childrearing practices to vary somewhat, and typically, within these classes. The observed variation is largely a function of education, income, urban–rural residence, and ethnic origin—factors that are often interrelated. Ethnic or national origin, which includes race, is usually associated with certain subcultural values and with the degree of discrimination or acceptance by the wider society. These variables, in turn, will promote or hinder educational and occupational achievement, and this will affect values—in the direction of the traditional or the modern.

Generally, the higher the class (except for the upper class, which is more conservative in certain respects), the more likely individuals are to adopt the modern values. Moreover, equalitarianism, rationalism, secularism, individualism, achievement, and tolerance are associated with declining sex typing and situational power in the relationship between the sexes. These qualities are associated with greater assertiveness in the female and greater expressiveness in the male.

Culturally defined conceptions of masculinity and femininity are learned by all classes, but the more educated classes are less rigidly bound by these traditions. They have greater freedom and more effective choices at work, at home, and at play. And they are freer to adopt personality traits and behavior that have been typed for the opposite sex.

There is more sharing and mutuality in the relationship between middle class men and women. Working class white men and women are more separated, psychologically and socially (40). Working class males feel more reluctance and shame about sharing in household tasks. They are more apt to segregate themselves from women in mixed groups, and they have fewer common nonerotic interests that they can discuss with women. The need to maintain the image of masculine toughness and command is stronger, and working class white men are less apt to be tender, sympathetic, and indulgent. The woman, on the other hand, tends to be more passive, nurturing, and emotionally volatile than her middle class counterpart (41).

As a rule, working class people are newer to the urban scene. They have less education, and they have less freedom on the job. The relative lack of autonomy on the job rubs off on all other areas of life, including the relationship between the sexes (42). Where conformity is a life style, experimentation, negotiation, and innovation do not thrive. Indeed, conformity tends to be more characteristic of the working class in all societies—even in America, the citadel of individualism.

The traditional belief in the inequality of the sexes is more strongly entrenched in the working class. Most working class women, when asked "Who is boss in your house?" will reply without hesitation "My husband." And they believe this. And yet, if we examine what actually goes on in the day-to-day operation of the household, we find that the working class woman has more real and effective authority than most middle class women. She will rent the apartment and select the furniture without consulting her husband, whereas a middle class woman rarely has this freedom. The working class male abdicates authority in most routine household decisions because of the survival of traditional patterns of separation in the interests and activities of the sexes. In situations of real conflict, however—major decisions about the use of extra income, serious disagreement about disciplining a child or about whether to move to a new neighborhood or city—the husband usually wins (43). If nothing else works, he may beat up his wife. It is largely for this reason that working class wives view their husbands as dominant and controlling. But their husbands have little education and few economic resources. The wife, less likely to have dropped out of school, may be more educated. If she works, her income may surpass that of her husband. It will certainly approach her husband's income more closely than in the middle class, where husbands tend to be more educated than their wives.

In the event of a divorce, middle class wives also have more to lose materially, particularly if they do not work. This factor, too, may diminish their authority in the home, relative to that of working class women. We do not know what the situation is in the upper class. Although upper class women are more familistic, they seem to have a great deal of freedom and independence

(44). Certainly if they have money of their own, they have many more options than their poorer contemporaries, even though they are less likely to choose careers and jobs as an outlet.

ETHNIC DIFFERENCES. Conceptions of masculinity and femininity, the degree of sex typing, and the authority relationships between the sexes vary also, and typically, within the various ethnic groups in the United States. Yet as individuals and families, through time, rise in the class structure, and as each succeeding generation becomes more highly educated and urbanized, such differences tend to disappear in the wake of increasing acculturation to the modern values. First-generation Americans (the original immigrants from foreign countries), and first-generation migrants from rural areas, are usually most patriarchal and traditional in their conceptions of masculinity and femininity. But this pattern varies according to the cultural heritage, the unique historical experiences of the group, and the current availability of educational and economic opportunities to various ethnic groups. This can be illustrated by examining the relationship between the sexes among American blacks, and within Japanese-, Mexican-, and Jewish-American subcultures in the United States today.

Black Americans. A distinctive element in the sexual identities of black women and men in the United States stems from the relative lack of a strong patriarchal tradition within the black subculture (45).

The West African areas, from which most slaves were taken, were patriarchal, but this heritage was largely destroyed when the slaves arrived on this continent. The independence of black women, furthermore, was promoted by the slave owners' practice of distributing food and other economic resources to the women. That is, males did not control and distribute these resources to their women and children. At the same time, a strong value was placed on males as breeding stock. Their sexual prowess increased the slave owners' supply of human property. For the same reason, slave women were not subject to the sexual repressions of the Judaeo-Christian heritage. Sexual freedom enhanced fertility. Legitimacy was irrelevant to the work potential of newborn slaves, and there was no property to pass on within black families.

Later, the fundamentalist religions attempted to regulate nonmarital sexual behavior among free blacks, but with less success than among other groups with a long heritage of the double standard. Furthermore, the greater ease with which black women were able to obtain employment (in domestic service) perpetuated the patterns of female self reliance and independence.

Today, black matriarchy does not exist in American society, any more than it has ever existed in any culture or subculture. Nevertheless, black males in all classes have less authority in the home than men of any other ethnic group (46). This does not mean that black women are unilaterally dominant, however, and they certainly are not in the middle class.

The relationship between the sexes in the black community differs from the traditional in other ways, also. Black working class males are more expressive in their relationships with women than is typical in the white working class. Mutual sexual gratification is somewhat more frequent. Black women are less conflicted about achieving and aspiring than white women. They have not been submerged within a patriarchal family structure for generations. Moreover, since the traditionally sextyped personality traits are less prevalent among both sexes, the potentials for mutuality, situational authority, and human realization are strong—given the existence of objective opportunity. Such potentials are apparent, particularly among more educated

blacks who have experienced some degree of economic and occupational success (47).

Jewish Americans. Jewish women in America also come from
a tradition in which women have had important economic provider roles. In the small towns or village shtetl communities of
Eastern Europe, from which most American Jews immigrated,
women often played the partner role (48). The Jews were a
commercial people, since they were forbidden to own land in
the Pale of Settlement in Eastern Europe, where they were confined by law. The modern values of achievement, rationalism,
and equalitarianism had long been part of the cultural heritage
of this group. Opportunities were limited by discrimination, but
some economic mobility was possible. In addition, the Jewish
religion fostered devotion to sacred learning, and Jewish women
often ran family commercial enterprises while their husbands
pursued the goal of religious learning.

After immigration to America, a continued active economic
role for women was encouraged by the tendency of American
Jews to enter occupations in which they could be self-employed.
The mama and the papa stores utilized the skills and energies of
both sexes in gainful occupations. And female descendents of
this immigrant group have tended to follow their fathers, their
brothers, and their husbands into college and into the traditional as well as the male-dominated professions.

Scattered studies of college and professional women have indicated that Jewish women have been more apt to be career-oriented than women of other religious origins. Jewish women, at
every economic level, are more likely to be gainfully employed
than white women of other religions (49). Sex typing along traditional lines is less prevalent within this group; partly because
Jewish men and women are predominantly middle class at this
point in their history in America. But the subcultural heritage of

American Jews, a heritage that emphasized many of the modern values even before immigration, has also been a significant factor in the present picture.

Japanese-Americans. In strong contrast to the experience of American blacks and Jews, the heritage of Japanese-Americans is more traditional with respect to sex typing and authority relationships between the sexes. This heritage, moreover, continues to affect the sexual identities of Japanese-American men and women.

The extreme authoritarianism and emphasis on female-to-male deference in traditional Japanese culture is reflected in recent studies in which oriental American women are found to have less authority within the home than women of any other group (50). The surviving traditional values that are still quite strong are a frequent source of conflict, especially for younger generations (51). The separation of the sexes in Japanese-American families is reinforced by the emphasis on familism, on unconditional obedience of wife and children, and on emotional reserve for both sexes. The continued existence of the extended family as a daily interacting unit for many Japanese-Americans helps preserve the separation of the sexes and extreme sex typing in behavior and activities.

Even in the third generation, comparisons between Japanese-Americans and other Americans of the same age indicate that Japanese-American males and females typically remain less overtly aggressive, more conforming, more emotionally reserved, and more sensitive to status distinctions (52). Changes in the direction of modern values are taking place, particularly among young, urban, educated, middle class Japanese-Americans. But tradition dies hard.

Mexican-Americans. Most Mexican-American men and women also live by and reflect traditional values in their personalities, modes of behavior, and authority relationships. The concept of machismo summarizes in one word the traditional ideal of masculinity in Mexican culture. Latin Americans happen to have a word to represent this complex of behavior, values, and attitudes. The conceptions, however, are not very different from conceptions of masculinity in most agricultural societies, and the same experiences that have begun to break down extreme sex typing and patriarchalism in other groups are operating for Mexican-Americans also.

Depending on whether Mexican-American men and women are poor and illiterate or well-off and educated, whether they live in rural or urban areas, whether they live in Texas or in more cosmopolitan Los Angeles, and whether they live in segregated barrios or in more diverse neighborhoods, sex typing and sexual identity vary on a continuum from the traditional to the modern (53).

Largely because of continuing discrimination and limited educational and economic opportunities, particularly in the rural areas of the border states, the traditional patterns are strong, even in the third generation after immigration. Most Mexican-American males believe it is shameful and a threat to their masculine pride to have an employed wife. Most continue to value high fertility and to oppose the use of birth control by their wives. Most Mexican-American women will tolerate a consensual union and their husband's infidelities.

The patterns just cited are not changing greatly, yet extended family households are rare in the large cities. Family visiting among younger generations is declining, and young Mexican-American men and women are beginning to turn to one another rather than to the extended family for help, advice, support, and psychological gratification.

Sex typing persists in American society, as a fact and as an ideal for most people. Most women continue to feel separate from and inferior to men—physically, emotionally, and intellectually.

The separate worlds of men and women are beginning to

merge, but the process is far from complete. Education and movement up the class structure helps. Government policy is important. Ethnic origin helps or hinders, depending on the historical traditions of the group and on other factors such as discrimination.

The term "unisex" refers to a clothing fad. It does not reflect the differences in sex-typed personality traits, goals, activities, and authority relationships of most men and women in American society today. Nor does it indicate the basic differences in self conceptions and identity that continue to separate the sexes, everywhere. But does it presage a change that will come as societies continue to automate and computerize? Are women a minority group—a group that will lose their minority status with time? If so, how will women's loss of minority status affect the sex-typed identities of men and women of the future?

Many characteristics that were believed to be inevitable in the identities and relationships between the sexes have turned out to be largely dependent on culture, time, and place. Can we predict, then, on the basis of probable developments in science and technology and the continued spread of modern values, the future roles and future identities of men and women? I think we can.

6 | Issues and Problems

The existence of a women's movement in many countries of the world means that at least some women, almost everywhere, feel that the changes in the identities and in the relationships between the sexes that have been taking place in most contemporary societies are proceeding too slowly.

Social movements arise and are led by groups who are experiencing change and, often, improvement in the circumstances of their lives. Rising expectations and increasing dissatisfaction go hand in hand. Seldom do the most miserable and downtrodden have the energy or the knowledge and insight to start social movements. They may revolt or riot; lacking communication, however, they do not engage in sustained and organized efforts to change themselves and the societies in which they live. Indeed, a major reason for the failure, throughout history, of isolated peasants to spawn or support more than a very few revolutions, was just such absence of communication—because of inadequate roads and impregnable geographic barriers, individuals could not be reached to be recruited.

The women's movement faces a similar problem. Roads are plentiful in technologically developed societies, as are communications media. Face-to-face contact, demonstrations, and other techniques for promoting support are hindered, however, by the isolation of most women within the family group. Leaders of the women's movement are usually single (never married) or divorced. They have the freedom to travel, speak, and recruit support and supporters. The masses of women, however, have not followed—not as yet, and certainly not in developing countries, where the great majority of women are not only isolated and bound to the family, but illiterate as well. They cannot be recruited by face-to-face contact or by the written word.

The success or failure of social movements depends largely on changing economic and political conditions. Losses in wars, economic depressions, and extreme differences in wealth are likely to strengthen social movements. Government reforms (usually granting token goals of the movement and mainly benefiting the more fortunate and coopted segments of the have-not population) and military suppression are likely to destroy social movements, at least temporarily.

It is not possible to predict the fate of the various women's movements around the world today. Much will depend on government policies and unpredictable world events. Whatever the future of the movement, in America and abroad, however, it will leave its mark in the changed consciousness of many women and men, particularly within more educated, urban groups.

Because the roles and problems of both women and men are being modified to some extent in many societies, an analysis of changing sexual identities throughout human history logically should end with a discussion of the major issue raised by the women's movement. This issue—the question of whether women are a minority group—is controversial, even among women. We can then turn to the question of the future sexual identities of men and women in all nations, classes, ethnic groups, and generations.

The two questions are related. If women are a minority group, this status is reflected in their authority relationships with men, in their sex-typed personality traits, and in the aspects of their respective identities or self images that result from learned conceptions of themselves as different and inferior in some ways to the male of the species.

WOMEN AS A MINORITY GROUP. Confusion about whether women are a minority group stems from a failure to define the concept of minority group accurately. The classic definition, and one that is often quoted, was formulated several decades ago by sociologist Louis Wirth: "A minority group is any group of people who, because of their physical or cultural characteristics, are singled out from others in the society in which they live for differential and unequal treatment, and who, therefore, regard themselves as objects of collective discrimination" (1).

The first part of Wirth's definition is correct. If a group of people, on the basis of physical traits that they cannot change (e.g., gender or race) or beliefs and values (e.g., religion) are automatically excluded from highly valued rewards and privileges in a society, that group is a minority group. This principle of reward and acceptance in a society rests on birth, primarily, rather than on merit or ability.

The second part of the definition, however, is not correct. Minority group status is an objective, measurable fact that does not necessarily include awareness of such status. Analogously, classes exist and can be located objectively, regardless of where individuals believe they belong in the class structure and regardless of what class they subjectively identify with. Consciousness raising, as a goal of the women's movement, rests on the recognition of the possibility that people may not be aware of their minority group status.

Given the first part of the definition, are women a minority group? The answer is obvious. Everywhere in the world, and regardless of official ideologies of those in power, women are largely excluded from the most highly rewarded and prestigious positions in government, industry, the church, and the professions. Only the entertainment field is open to them, as it is to members of other minority groups. And even here, women must often trade erotic favors for advancement.

In the occupational world, in the United States, women who work full-time earn about one-third less than men in the same field. They are more likely to be employed at lower levels, as well (e.g., as teachers rather than as principals) (2). Women are much less apt to be promoted than men, and they are much less likely to hold positions of leadership and authority—particularly over men.

Furthermore, women's access to highly valued positions in the United States has been declining (3). Comparing statistics from other countries with data from the United States, we find that the exclusion of women from top level occupations is more severe in this country than in many other industrialized or industrializing countries. Women in America are more likely to be in middle level white collar occupations, however, since there are more of these jobs available in the United States economy.

The minority group status of women is indicated in other ways also. The sex-typed personality traits of women in the direction of passivity, dependence, and submissiveness are not highly valued in industrialized societies. Psychotherapists, in fact, tend to equate these traits with neurosis, particularly if they occur in men (4). Women have less authority in their relationships with men, even if they have equal resources, and sometimes even if they have more resources (5). A number of studies have demonstrated women's greater desire to have been born a member of the opposite sex, their lower self esteem (particularly when they are not gainfully employed), and their tendency to judge other women more harshly than they judge men, especially when these women are their employers or their teachers.

Most women prefer men in positions of authority. In the past, Gallup polls have found repeatedly that women would be far less likely than men to vote for a qualified woman to be president of the United States. This attitude appears to have changed recently, however. In a poll conducted by Louis Harris in 1971, women were more likely than men to say they would vote for a qualified woman to be president, although the number of either sex who would do so was small—17 per cent of the women respondents and 7 per cent of the men who were polled (6). Previously, then, women were more prejudiced against women, in certain respects, than men were, and this too helped perpetuate their minority status.

The creative and academic contributions of women are undervalued relative to those of men. In one study, when women students were asked to judge the merit of papers falsely attributed to women authors, they judged these papers more harshly than those they believed to be written by men (7). Students also prefer male to female college professors and attribute greater competence to their male professors (8). Yet because of discrimination and a much more rigorous selective process, women professors tend to score higher than male professors, on the average, on tests of academic and intellectual ability (9).

It is sometimes argued that women are not a minority group since they own most of the national wealth. (Wealthy widows have inherited from their husbands, who often predecease them because the men were older in the first place.) However, women do not own the majority of individually owned shares in the United States. Their ownership of property, furthermore, is often in name only, to allow families to obtain income tax benefits. But most important, women do not translate economic wealth into power. They are barely visible in nationwide decision-making bodies in government and industry.

In many ways, women in America suffer the same disabilities as American blacks, a similarity that has been noted by a number of writers, among them Gunnar Myrdal in his classic study, *The American Dilemma,* and Helen Hacker (10). If we use an objective definition of minority group status, the question shifts from "Are women a minority group?" to "Why are women a mi-

nority group in modern societies?" Clearly they were not minor-
ities in hunting and gathering societies—even less in horticultural societies, particularly those that had matrilineal family
forms. Indisputably, too, the shifting status of women, historically and cross culturally, has been very closely related to technological development and to the changing economic roles of
women.

Women in modern times have not shared the economic provider role equally with men; nor do they have the prestige they
have enjoyed in other societies. As their ancillary economic
functions and their functions as teachers and healers were taken
over by factories and professionals, women did not move their
base of activities from the family to the industrial and service
economy, proportionately. They did not share equally in the
shift of protective and distributive functions (the redistribution
of income through taxation) from the family to government. Sex
typing in personality—emphasizing dependence, passivity, and
obedience for women—became more extreme in agricultural societies. Authority relations between men and women grew more
patriarchal. As industrialization proceeded, women became less
suited psychologically for extrafamilial functioning, and men became increasingly overburdened, physically and psychologically, in their role as sole economic provider. The consequences
(e.g., in the broadening gap between male and female life expectancies) are not as well known or appreciated as they should
be. The costs to men, women, and society have only recently
been documented by Jessie Bernard and other social critics (11).

In the course of human history, women shifted from the equal
partner role in hunting and gathering societies to varying forms
of the junior or silent partner role. If they can return to the
equal partner role—equal in prestige, power, and possession of
valued resources—men will be released from unfair burdens,
and women will be freed from wasteful restrictions on their talents and abilities.

The almost total exclusion of women from the highest positions of power and privilege in the nonfamily sphere in modern societies rests partly on the continued existence of sex typing in childrearing practices. Exclusionist practice is reinforced by the work structure in industrial societies—with emphasis on full-time employment and geographic mobility. It is promoted by the continuation of the traditional separation of functions and the traditional division of labor within the family in most contemporary societies. Almost everywhere, governments have underwritten the last-named circumstance by failing to extend their health, education, and welfare functions to include adequate infant and child care services.

The continued emphasis on the traditional roles and personality traits, and the persistence of sex-typed identities among women, are basic factors in the virtual exclusion of women from higher level occupations. Most women would not seek such positions even if they were accessible to them. They do not view themselves as tough enough, independent enough, or competent enough. Furthermore, most women could not give the commitment in time and energy required by these occupations at the present time. The failure to provide adequate child care facilities for the children of working mothers, the full-time structuring of most jobs, and the travel requirements of high level jobs, greatly hinder the women who do seek outlets in nonfamily activities.

The situation just described will not change greatly until childrearing practices in which gender is regarded as irrelevant to the abilities, personalities, and activities of human beings become typical for all groups. But personality and identity continue to change throughout the life cycle, and current modifications due to developments in science and technology and the rise of the women's movement will have immediate and ultimate effects on values and attitudes which are not readily observable in the actual life circumstances of most women.

In the United States, blacks, increasingly, are viewing themselves as beautiful; women increasingly are viewing themselves as strong, competent, independent, and resourceful. Identity and behavior are two aspects of the same coin. Changing roles, as economic and educational opportunities increase, affect identity; changing identity—changing self conceptions and self evaluations—affects the goals that women strive for (four children, a station wagon, and a home in the suburbs or a Ph.D.) and the means that they use to achieve these goals (glamour aids or education).

FUTURE SEXUAL IDENTITIES.   The notion of cultural pluralism, the tolerance and preference for many alternative life styles in complex societies, has yet to be applied to the functions and activities of men and women. But this is a logical extension of the principle. It will be underwritten by continued developments in technology and science and by the continued spread of the modern values among increasingly educated people in all societies.

Science and technology can destroy, but they can also liberate. They provide alternatives and choices. They foster rationalism and individualism. They promote change, which in turn encourages self reliance and independence for both sexes. The increasingly high level of education required to function in technologically developed societies fosters openness to change. Permissive childrearing, which focuses on the human being, regardless of gender, promotes independence, warmth, and expressiveness in all people—again, regardless of gender.

Most women in present-day America are gainfully employed, at least during certain periods of their lives. Eventually all women who are physically and mentally able will very likely work continuously from the time they complete their education until they reach retirement age. Their working hours will be shorter—equivalent to what is now defined as part-time work. Adequate day care facilities, operated by trained professionals, will be universally available during the hours of the shorter work week. Retirement ages will be lower. There will be more jobs to choose from, particularly in the health, education, and welfare fields, as all societies—democratic, socialist, and oligarchic—become total welfare states. Moreover, jobs that are available will be equally shared by men and women. The length of the work week, the degree of commitment, and the rewards earned will not vary on the basis of sex.

These predictions are speculative, but they are a logical extension of current trends in science, technology, economics, childrearing practices, sex typing, and sexual identity. If little girls are going to grow up to share the provider role equally with men, parents will need to encourage assertiveness, independence, and competence in all their children, regardless of sex.

The greater material comforts produced by advanced technologies will continue to diminish the strength of the work ethic. Men will become less and less possessive about the sole provider role. They will value success less and their families more—particularly as purchasing power continues to increase and materialism declines. In the early 1970s a large majority of young people, polled in a nationwide sample (12), answered "Yes" to the question: "Could you accomplish more each day if you tried?" Older people more frequently replied "No." College students, asked about their major concerns, listed the family and problems of maintaining and strengthening family life above all other concerns (13).

Given the greater importance of the husband–wife rather than the parent–child tie in modern societies, mutuality becomes central to the man–woman relationship. It promotes sharing of all activities—childrearing, homemaking, and breadwinning. This does not imply a role reversal, but simply a mutual identification and a mutual desire to help one another.

With the continued spread of individualism, humanism, and equalitarianism in modern societies, the commodity view of human beings begins to disappear. Eventually women will cease to be viewed as sexual commodities, and men will no longer be evaluated as economic commodities—according to their earning power. The terms masculinity and femininity will disappear from modern languages because they will no longer reflect standards that guide thought, emotion, and behavior. The primary source for such standards will be the individual and his or her temperament and abilities—these factors alone will determine the roles and the identities of all human beings, regardless of gender. When this change has been achieved, all humans will be liberated. This is the latest, and perhaps the last, psychological frontier.

Notes

CHAPTER 2

1. Eleanor E. Maccoby (ed.), *The Development of Sex Differences*, Stanford University Press, Palo Alto, Calif., 1966.
2. See Inge K. Broverman et al., "Sex-Role Stereotypes: A Current Appraisal," *Journal of Social Issues*, 28: 59–78, 1972.
3. See Ashley Montagu, *The Natural Superiority of Women*, Macmillan, New York, 1968; B. Childs, "Genetic Origins of Some Sex Differences Among Human Beings," *Pediatrics*, 35: 798–812, 1965; J. M. Tanner, *Growth at Adolescence*, 2nd ed., Charles C. Thomas, Springfield, Ill., 1962.
4. Johannes Nielsen, "Klinefelter's Syndrome and the XYY Syndrome," *Acta Psychiatrica Scandinavica*, 1969, Supplement 209; M. D. Casey, D. R. Street, L. J. Segall, and C. E. Blank, "Patients with Sex Chromatin Abnormality in Two State Hospitals," *Annals of Human Genetics*, 32: 53–63, 1968.
5. Unpublished study by Eugene Lewit, National Bureau of Economic Research, 1971.
6. Judith M. Bardwick, *The Psychology of Women*, Harper & Row, New York, 1971, p. 46.
7. Clellan S. Ford and Frank A. Beach, *Patterns of Sexual Behavior*, Harper & Row, New York, 1951 p. 259.
8. *Ibid.*, p. 27.
9. Robert W. Goy, "Organizing Effect of Androgen on the Behavior of Rhesus Monkeys," in Richard P. Michael (ed.), *Endocri-*

197

nology and Human Behavior, Oxford University Press, London, 1968; also Milton Diamond (ed.), *Perspectives in Reproduction and Sexual Behavior,* Indiana University Press, Bloomington, 1968.

10. See, for example, David A. Hamburg and Donald T. Lunde, "Sex Hormones in the Development of Sex Differences in Human Behavior," in Maccoby, *op. cit.,* pp. 1–24; also John Money and Anke A. Ehrhardt, "Prenatal Hormone Exposure: Possible Effects on Behavior in Man," in Michael, *op. cit.,* Chapter 3.

11. Irven De Vore (ed.), *Primate Behavior,* Holt, Rinehart & Winston, New York, 1965; also Harriet L. Rheingold (ed.), *Maternal Behavior in Mammals,* Wiley, New York, 1963.

12. Richard Green and John Money, *Transsexualism and Sex Reassignment,* Johns Hopkins Press, Baltimore, 1969; John Money and Anke A. Ehrhardt, *Man and Woman Boy and Girl,* Johns Hopkins Press, Baltimore, 1972.

13. See, for example, Robert Ardrey, *The Territorial Imperative,* Atheneum, New York, 1966; also Konrad Lorenz, *On Aggression,* Harcourt Brace Jovanovich, New York, 1963.

14. For a review of evidence on the lack of a genetic basis for human aggression by a variety of experts from different fields, see M. F. Ashley Montagu (ed.), *Man and Aggression,* Oxford University Press, New York, 1968.

15. Margaret Mead, *Sex and Temperament in Three Primitive Societies,* Morrow, New York, 1935.

16. *Ibid.,* p. 42.

17. *Ibid.,* p. 113.

18. For a comprehensive review of data on the general topic of biological rhythms, see Gay Gaer Luce, *Biological Rhythms in Psychiatry and Medicine,* U.S. Government Printing Office, Washington, D.C., 1970. This report also contains an excellent bibliography.

19. A summary of much recent data on this topic can be found in Bardwick, *op. cit.,* Chapter II.

20. Luce, *op. cit.,* pp. 110–111.

21. Glenn D. Wilson, "An Electrodermal Technique for the Study of Phobia," *New England Journal of Medicine,* 85: 696–698, 1966.

22. Albertina A. Weinlander, "Sex Differences in Scores on the Structured-Objective Rorschach Test," *Psychological Reports,* 18: 839–842, 1966; B. N. Phillips, "Defensiveness as a Factor in Sex Differences in Anxiety," *Journal of Consulting Psychology,* 30: 167–169, 1966.

23. These studies are reviewed by Roy G. D'Andrade, "Sex Differences and Cultural Institutions," in Maccoby, *op. cit.,* pp. 173–203.

24. Leo Srole, Thomas S. Langner, Stanley T. Nueball, Marvin K. Opler, and Thomas A. C. Rennie, *Mental Health in the Metropolis,* McGraw-Hill, New York, 1962.

25. Pauline Bart, *Depression in Middle Aged Women,* Schenkman, Boston, in press.

26. Ford and Beach, *op. cit.,* p. 113.

27. Mary Jane Sherfey, *The Nature and Evolution of Female Sexuality,* Random House, New York, 1972, p. 140.

28. *Ibid.,* p. 111.

29. *Ibid.,* pp. 112–113.

30. Ford and Beach, *op. cit.,* p. 87.

31. William Masters and Virginia Johnson, "The Clitoris: Anatomic and Clinical Considerations," in John Money (ed.), *Sex Research: New Developments,* Holt, Rinehart & Winston, 1965; also William Masters and Virginia Johnson, *Human Sexual Response,* Little, Brown, Boston, 1966, p. 65.

32. Ford and Beach, *op. cit.,* p. 113.

33. Erik H. Erikson, "Inner and Outer Space: Reflections on Womanhood," in Robert Jay Lifton (ed.), *The Woman in America,* Houghton Mifflin, Boston, 1965, pp. 2–26.

34. These ideas were developed primarily in three papers: "Some Psychical Consequences of the Anatomical Distinction Between the Sexes," in James Strachey (ed.), *The Standard Edition of the Complete Psychological Works of Sigmund Freud,* Hogarth Press, London, 1965–1966, Vol. XIX, pp. 248–258; "Female Sexuality," *ibid.,* Vol. XXI, pp. 225–243; and "Femininity," *ibid.,* Vol. XXII, pp. 112–135.

35. For a bibliography of a number of studies on this topic, see Roberta M. Oetzel, Annotated Bibliography, in Maccoby, *op. cit.,* pp. 346–347.

36. Freud, "Femininity," *op. cit.*, Vol. XXII, p. 118.

37. *Ibid.*, p. 116.

38. *Ibid.*, p. 114.

39. Freud, "Some Psychical Consequences of the Anatomical Distinction Between the Sexes," *op. cit.*, Vol. XIX, p. 258.

40. Bruno Bettelheim, "The Commitment Required of a Woman Entering a Scientific Profession in Present-Day American Society," in Jacquelyn A. Mattfeld and Carol G. Van Aken, *Women and the Scientific Professions*, M.I.T. Press Cambridge, Mass., 1965, p. 15.

41. Bruno Bettelheim, *Symbolic Wounds*, rev. ed., Free Press, New York, 1962.

42. *Ibid.*, p. 111.

43. *Ibid.*, p. 151.

44. Freud, "Female Sexuality," *op. cit.*, Vol. XXI, p. 228.

45. See, for example, Robert R. Bell, "Some Factors Related to the Sexual Satisfaction of the College Educated Wife," *Family Life Coordinator*, 13: 43–47, 1964; Lee Rainwater, "Marital Sexuality in Four Cultures of Poverty," *Journal of Marriage and the Family*, 26: 457–466, 1964; Paul H. Gebhard, "Postmarital Coitus Among Widows and Divorcees," in Paul Bohannan (ed.), *Divorce and After*, Doubleday, Garden City, N.Y., 1970, pp. 81–96; Paul H. Gebhard, "Factors in Marital Orgasm," *Journal of Social Issues*, 22: 88–95, 1966.

46. Masters and Johnson, *op. cit.*, 1966, p. 263.

47. Ford and Beach, *op. cit.*, p. 94.

48. Natalie Shainess, "Psychological Problems Associated with Motherhood," in Silvano Arieti (ed.), *American Handbook of Psychiatry*, Vol. 2, Basic Books, New York, 1966, pp. 47–65.

49. Arthur R. Jensen, "How Much Can We Boost I.Q. and Scholastic Achievement?" *Harvard Educational Review*, 39: 1–123, 1969.

50. See, for example, Patricia W. Lunneborg, "Sex Differences in Aptitude Maturation During College," *Journal of Counseling Psychology*, 16: 463–464, 1969.

51. Herbert Spencer (1873), *The Study of Sociology*, University of Michigan Press, Ann Arbor, 1961, pp. 341–342.

52. See, for example, Havelock Ellis, *Man and Woman*, 4th ed., Scribner, New York, 1908; Gregorio Maranon, *The Evolution of Sex and Intersexual Conditions*, Allen & Unwin, London, 1932; Joseph E. Garai and Amram Scheinfeld, "Sex Differences in Mental and Behavioral Traits," *Genetic Psychology Monographs*, 77: 169–299, 1968.

CHAPTER 3

1. A number of investigators have viewed technological development as the major factor in determining social change. See particularly V. Gordon Childe, *Man Makes Himself*, Mentor, New York, 1951, and *What Happened in History*, Penguin, Baltimore, 1964; William F. Ogburn, *Social Change*, Viking, New York, 1922, and *Technology and the Changing Family*, Houghton Mifflin, Boston, 1955; and Gerhard Lenski, *Human Societies*, McGraw-Hill, New York, 1970.

2. A classic example of this approach is Frederick Engels (1884), *The Origin of the Family, Private Property and the State*, International Publishers, New York, 1972. With an introduction and notes by Eleanor Burke Leacock.

3. For this definition of power see Max Weber, *From Max Weber: Essays in Sociology*, Oxford University Press, New York, 1946, p. 180. Translated, edited, and with an introduction by Hans H. Gerth and C. Wright Mills.

4. For discussion or applications of this theory of power, see John R. P. French, Jr., and Bertram Raven, "The Bases of Social Power," in *Studies in Social Power*, Institute for Social Research, Ann Arbor, 1959, pp. 150–165; Paul F. Secord and Carl W. Backman, *Social Psychology*, McGraw-Hill, New York, 1964; Robert O. Blood, Jr., and Donald M. Wolfe, *Husbands and Wives*, Free Press, New York, 1960; John Scanzoni, *Sexual Bargaining*, Prentice-Hall, Englewood Cliffs, N.J., 1972.

5. Jerold Heiss and Charles F. Noll, *Aspects of Black Family Life*, Columbia University Press, New York, in press.

6. Willard Waller, *The Family: A Dynamic Interpretation*, Cordon, New York, 1938.

7. Meyer F. Nimkoff and Russell Middleton, "Types of Family and Types of Economy," *The American Journal of Sociology*, 66: 215–225, 1966; Rae Lesser Blumberg and Robert F. Winch, "Societal Complexity and Familial Complexity: Evidence for the Curvilinear Hypothesis," *The American Journal of Sociology*, 77: 898–920, 1972.

8. George Peter Murdock, *Social Structure*, Free Press, Glencoe, Ill., 1949, pp. 36–37; also Dwight B. Heath, "Sexual Division of Labor and Cross-Cultural Research," *Social Forces*, 37: 77–79, 1958; and Kathleen Gough, "The Origin of the Family," *Journal of Marriage and the Family*, 33: 760–770, 1971.

9. See E. E. Evans-Pritchard, *The Position of Women in Primitive Societies and Other Essays in Social Anthropology*, Faber and Faber, London, 1965; Clellan S. Ford, "Some Primitive Societies," in Georgene Seward and Robert C. Williamson (eds.), *Sex Roles in Changing Society*, Random House, Hew York, 1970, pp. 25–43.

10. F. Young and A. Bacadayan, "Menstrual Taboos and Social Rigidity," *Ethnology*, 4: 225–240, 1965.

11. Roy G. D'Andrade, "Sex Differences and Cultural Institutions," in Eleanor E. Maccoby (ed.), *The Development of Sex Differences*, Stanford University Press, Palo Alto, Calif., 1966, p. 201.

12. Herbert Barry, III, Margaret K. Bacon, and Irvin L. Child, "A Cross Cultural Survey of Some Sex Differences in Socialization," *Journal of Abnormal and Social Psychology*, 55: 327–332, 1957.

13. See Michael Young and Peter Willmott, *Family and Kinship in East London*, Routledge & Kegan Paul, London, 1957.

14. Max Weber (1922), *The Sociology of Religion*, Beacon, Boston 1963. Translated by Ephraim Fishoff.

15. Mary Beard, *Women as a Force in History*, Macmillan, New York, 1946.

16. Women's Bureau, *Profile of the Woman Worker: Fifty Years of Progress*, U.S. Government Printing Office, Washington, D.C., 1970; Women's Bureau, *Background Facts on Women Workers in the United States*, U.S. Government Printing Office, Washington, D.C., 1970.

17. Robert O. Blood, Jr., and Donald M. Wolfe, *op. cit.*

18. Margaret M. Paloma and T. Neal Garland, "The Myth of the Equalitarian Family: Familial Roles and the Professionally Em-

ployed Wife," in Athena Theodore (ed.), *The Professional Woman,* Schenkman, Boston, 1971, pp. 741–761.

19. Reported in *The New York Times,* April 10, 1972, p. 1.

20. See Clifford Kirkpatrick, *The Family as Process and Institution,* Ronald, New York, 1963, pp. 448–462, for a similar but more elaborate analysis.

21. See Lynda Lytle Holmstrom, *The Two-Career Family,* Schenkman, Boston, 1972.

22. John Scanzoni, *Sexual Bargaining,* Prentice-Hall, Englewood Cliffs, N.J., 1972.

23. Women's Bureau, *Background Facts on Women Workers in the United States, op. cit.*

24. Will Durant, *The Story of Civilization: The Life of Greece,* Simon & Schuster, New York, 1939; George Glasgow, *The Minoans,* Jonathan Cape, London, 1923.

25. H. D. F. Kotto, *The Greeks,* Penguin, Baltimore, 1960; Hans Licht, *Sexual Life in Ancient Greece,* Barnes & Noble, New York, 1963; W. K. Lacey, *The Family in Classical Greece,* Cornell University Press, Ithaca, N.Y., 1968.

26. Georgene H. Seward, "Sex Roles, Ancient to Modern," in Georgene H. Seward and Robert C. Williamson (eds.), *Sex Roles in Changing Society, op. cit.,* pp. 109–125.

27. Philip E. Slater, *The Glory of Hera,* Beacon, Boston, 1968, p. 8.

28. I Corinthians 11:3–10.

29. Hugo G. Beigel, "Romantic Love," *American Sociological Review,* 16: 326–334, 1951.

30. Frank E. Furstenburg, "Industrialization and the American Family: A Look Backward," *American Sociological Review,* 31: 65–72, 1966.

31. See Arthur W. Calhoun, *A Social History of the American Family,* Vol. I, Barnes & Noble, New York, 1945.

32. See Francis L. K. Hsu, *Under the Ancestors' Shadow: Chinese Culture and Personality,* Columbia University Press, New York, 1948; Marion J. Levy, Jr., *The Family Revolution in Modern China,* Harvard University Press, Cambridge, Mass., 1949; Maurice Freedman (ed.), *Family and Kinship in Chinese Society,* Stanford University Press, Palo Alto, Calif., 1970.

33. William J. Goode, *World Revolution and Family Patterns*, Free Press, New York, 1963, pp. 309–312.

34. See Ruth Benedict, *The Chrysanthemum and the Sword: Patterns of Japanese Culture*, Houghton Mifflin, Boston, 1946; Robert J. Smith and Richard K. Beardsley (eds.), *Japanese Culture: Its Development and Characteristics*, Aldine, Chicago, 1962; George De Vos, *The Heritage of Endurance*, University of California Press, Berkeley, 1971.

35. Several good sources on the traditional Indian family are: McKim Marriott (ed.), *Village India*, University of Chicago Press, Chicago, 1955; K. M. Kapadia, *Marriage and Family in India*, Oxford University Press, Bombay, India, 1959; M. S. Gore, "The Traditional Indian Family," in Meyer F. Nimkoff, *Comparative Family Systems*, Houghton Mifflin, Boston, 1965, pp. 209–231. See also Aileen D. Ross, *The Hindu Family in its Urban Setting*, University of Toronto Press, Toronto, Canada, 1961, for an analysis of change from traditional to transitional forms.

36. See Monroe Berger, *The Arab World Today*, Doubleday, Garden City, N.Y., 1962; William Goode, *World Revolution and Family Patterns, op. cit.*, Chapter III; Louise E. Sweet (ed.), *Peoples and Cultures of the Middle East*, Natural History Press, New York, 1970; David Miller and Clark D. Moore, *The Middle East: Yesterday and Today*, Bantam, New York, 1970.

37. See Esther Boserup, *Women's Role in Economic Development*, St. Martin's Press, New York, 1970.

CHAPTER 4

1. Ruth Sidel, *Women and Child Care in China*, Hill & Wang, New York, 1972.

2. Donald R. Brown (ed.), *The Role and Status of Women in the Soviet Union*, Teachers College Press, New York, 1968.

3. Edmund Dahlstrom (ed.), *The Changing Roles of Men and Women*, Beacon, Boston, 1971.

4. Dorwin L. Thomas and Andrew J. Weigert, "Socialization and Adolescent Conformity to Significant Others," *American Sociological Review*, 36: 835–847, 1971; Georgene H. Seward and

Robert C. Williamson, "A Cross-National Study of Adolescent Professional Goals," *Human Development*, 11: 248–254, 1969.

5. Hans L. Zetterberg, *On Sexual Life in Sweden*, Swedish Institute of Opinion Research, Sweden, 1968.

6. Sidel, *op. cit.*, p. 35.

7. For recent observations of changes in mainland China by a number of *New York Times* correspondents, see *Report From Red China*, Avon, New York, 1972.

8. See Jan Myrdal, *Report From a Chinese Village*, Random, New York, 1965.

9. See Takashi Kayama, *The Changing Social Position of Women in Japan*, UNESCO, Paris, 1961.

10. See Robert Blood, *Love Match and Arranged Marriage*, Free Press, New York, 1967.

11. For a review of Soviet government policy toward the family see Kent Geiger, "The Soviet Family," in Meyer F. Nimkoff (ed.), *Comparative Family Systems*, Houghton Mifflin, Boston, 1965, pp. 301–328; Urie Bronfenbrenner, "The Changing Soviet Family," in Brown, *op. cit.*, pp. 98–124; See also, Mark G. Field and Karin I. Flynn, "Worker, Mother, Housewife: Soviet Woman Today," in Georgene H. Seward and Robert C. Williamson (eds.), *Sex Roles in Changing Society*, Random House, New York, 1970, pp. 257–284; and Rose Somerville, "The Urban Working Woman in the U.S.S.R.: An Historical Overview," in André Michel (ed.), *Family Issues in Europe and America*, E. J. Brill, Leiden, 1971, pp. 91–103.

12. Boris Urlanis, "Some Demographic Trends," in G. P. Osipov (ed.), *Studies in Soviet Society: Town, Country and People*, Tavistock, London, 1969, pp. 41–53.

13. Reported in *The New York Times*, May 6, 1972, p. 3.

14. See F. Ivan Nye and Lois Wladis Hoffman, *The Employed Mother in America*, Rand McNally, Chicago, 1963.

15. Urie Bronfenbrenner, *Two Worlds of Childhood*, Russell Sage Foundation, New York, 1970, p. 15.

16. See Robert O. Blood, Jr., "The Effect of the Wife's Employment on the Husband–Wife Relationship," in Jerold Heiss (ed.), *Family Roles and Interaction*, Rand McNally, Chicago, 1968, pp. 255–269.

17. Cynthia F. Epstein, *Women's Place*, University of California Press, Berkeley, 1970, p. 7; Dean D. Knudsen, "The Declining Status of Women: Popular Myths and the Failure of Functionalist Thought," *Social Forces*, 48: 183–193, 1969.

18. See Virginia Olesen, "Leads on Old Questions from a New Revolution: Notes on Cuban Women, 1969," in Cynthia Fuchs Epstein and William J. Goode (eds.), *The Other Half*, Prentice-Hall, Englewood Cliffs, N.J., 1971, pp. 134–142.

19. See Hannah Papanak, "Purdah in Pakistan: Seclusion in Modern Occupations for Women," *Journal of Marriage and the Family*, 33: 517–30, 1970.

20. Several recent or still applicable sources on the status of women in Latin America and Spain are: Robert C. Williamson, "Role Themes in Latin America," in Seward and Williamson, *op. cit.*, pp. 177–199; Levy Cruz, "Brazil," in Raphael Patai (ed.), *Women in the Modern World*, Free Press, New York, 1967, pp. 209–226; Mercedes F. de Careaga, "Spain," in Patai, *ibid.*, pp. 176–191; Oscar Lewis, *Five Families*, Basic Books, New York, 1959; Ann Pescatello (ed.), *Male and Female in Latin America*, University of Pittsburgh Press, Pittsburgh, 1972; Nora Scott Kinzer, "Priests, Machos and Babies: Or Latin American Women and the Manichaean Heresy," *Journal of Marriage and the Family*, 35: 300–312, 1973.

21. See Stanislav Andreski, *Parasitism and Subversion: The Case of Latin America*, Pantheon, New York, 1966.

22. Lewis, *op. cit.;* also Oscar Lewis, *La Vida*, Random House, New York, 1965.

23. See Leo Grebler, Joan W. Moore, and Ralph C. Guzman, *The Mexican American People*, Free Press, New York, 1970, Chapter 15; also, John W. Moore with Alfredo Cuellar, *Mexican Americans*, Prentice-Hall, Englewood Cliffs, N.J., 1970, Chapter 6.

24. Paula H. Hass, "Maternal Role Incompatibility and Fertility in Urban Latin America," *The Journal of Social Issues*, 28: 111–127, 1972.

25. See *Report on Women and Girls in National Development*, UNICEF, New York, 1972.

26. For a description of changing values in a Turkish village as promoted by industrialization, see Paul J. Magnarella, "Conjugal Role-Relationships in a Modernizing Turkish Town," *International Journal of Sociology of the Family*, 2: 179–192, 1972.

27. Mary Diamenti, "Sparkling Glasses on a Shelf," UNICEF, New York, 1972, p. 4.

28. See Daniel Lerner, *The Passing of Traditional Society*, Free Press, New York, 1958.

29. A. Hussein, "The Family as a Social Unit—Responsibilities of Husband and Wife." Paper presented at the Eighth Conference of the International Planned Parenthood Federation, Santiago, Chile, 1967.

30. Mirra Komarovsky, "Cultural Contradictions and Sex Roles: The Masculine Case," *American Sociological Review*, 78: 873–884, 1973.

31. Several older but excellent sources on Africa are: George P. Murdock, *Africa*, McGraw-Hill, New York, 1959; Simon and Phoebe Ottenburg, *Cultures and Societies of Africa*, Random House, New York 1960. See also, Remi Clignet, *Many Wives, Many Powers*, Northwestern University Press, Evansten, Ill., 1970; Iris Andreski, *Old Wives' Tales: Life Stories of African Women*, Schocken, New York, 1970.

32. See Elizabeth Hunting Wheeler, "Sub-Saharan Africa," in Patai, *op. cit.*, pp. 317–345.

33. Margaret Dobert and Nwangango Shields, "Africa's Women: Security and Challenge in Change," *Africa Report*, 17: 14–20, 1972.

34. William Goode, *World Revolution and Family Patterns*, Free Press, New York, 1963.

35. Alfred Katzenstein, "Male and Female in the German Democratic Republic," in Seward and Williamson, *op. cit.*, pp. 240–256.

36. Inge K. Broverman, Susan R. Vogel, Donald M. Broverman, Frank E. Clarkson, and Paul S. Rosencrantz, "Sex Role Stereotypes: A Current Appraisal," *Journal of Social Issues*, 28: 59–78, 1972.

CHAPTER 5

1. See Everett Hughes, "Dilemmas and Contradictions of Status," *American Journal of Sociology*, 50: 353–359, 1945; Shirley Angrist, "The Study of Sex Roles," *Journal of Social Issues*, 25: 215–232, 1969.

2. Joseph E. Garai and Amram Scheinfeld, "Sex Differences in Mental and Behavioral Traits," *Genetic Psychology Monographs*, 77: 169–299, 1968.

3. For references on a number of the generalizations about male and female personality differences discussed in this chapter, see Eleanor E. Maccoby (ed.), *The Development of Sex Differences*, Stanford University Press, Palo Alto, Calif., 1966; Judith Bardwick, *The Psychology of Women*, Harper & Row, New York, 1971; Julia A. Sherman, *On the Psychology of Women*, Charles C. Thomas, Springfield, Ill., 1971. Two excellent review articles of recent research in this area are: Lois Wladis Hoffman, "Childhood Experiences and Achievement," *Journal of Social Issues*, 28: 129–155, 1972; and Arlie Hochschild, "A Review of Sex Role Research," *American Journal of Sociology*, 78: 1011–1029, 1973.

4. David C. McClelland, J. W. Atkinson, R. A. Clark, and E. L. Lowell, *The Achievement Motive*, Appleton-Century-Crofts, New York, 1953; see also, Bernard C. Rosen, H. J. Crockett, Jr., and C. Z. Nunn (eds.), *Achievement in American Society*, Schenkman, Cambridge, Mass., 1969.

5. Matina Horner, *Sex Differences in Achievement Motivation and Performance in Competive and Non-Competitive Situations*. Doctoral dissertation, University of Michigan, Ann Arbor, 1968.

6. Matina Horner, "The Motive to Avoid Success and Changing Aspirations of College Women," in Judith Bardwicke, *Readings on the Psychology of Women*, Harper & Row, 1972, pp. 62–67; also Peter J. Weston and Martha Mednick, "Race, Social Class, and the Motive to Avoid Success in Women," *Journal of Cross Cultural Psychology*, 1: 284–291, 1970.

7. Reported by Lois Wladis Hoffman in "The Professional Woman as Mother." Paper presented at the Conference on Successful Women in the Sciences, New York Academy of Science, New York, 1972.

8. See Edward A. Suchman, "The 'Hang-Loose' Ethic and the Spirit of Drug Use," *Journal of Health and Social Behavior*, 9: 146–155, 1968.

9 Jerome Kagan and Howard A. Moss, *Birth to Maturity*, Wiley, New York, 1962.

10. For a summary of the negative conclusions reached in a number of these earlier studies of the happiness and mental health of ca-

reer women, see Edwin C. Lewis, *Developing Women's Potential*, Iowa State University Press, Ames, 1968.

11. Lois Wladis Hoffman, "Childhood Experiences and Achievement," *op. cit.*, p. 146.

12. Sandra Schwartz Tangri, *Role Innovation in Occupational Choice Among College Women*. Doctoral dissertation, University of Michigan, Ann Arbor, 1969; Ravenna Helson, "The Changing Image of the Career Woman," *Journal of Social Issues*, 28: 33–46, 1972.

13. Jerome Kagan, "Acquisition and Significance of Sex Typing and Sex Role Identity," in Martin L. Hoffman and Lois Wladis Hoffman (eds.), *Review of Child Development Research*, Vol. I., Russell Sage Foundation, New York, 1964; Bernard C. Rosen, "Family Structure and Value Transmission," *Merrill-Palmer Quarterly*, 10: 59-76, 1964; Eleanor E. Maccoby, "The Development of Moral Values and Behavior in Childhood, in John A. Clausen (ed.), *Socialization and Society*, Little, Brown, Boston, 1968, pp. 227–269; Dorwin L. Thomas and Andrew J. Weigert, "Socialization and Adolescent Conformity to Significant Others," *American Sociological Review*, 36: 835–847, 1971.

14. I. Iscoe, M. Williams, and J. Harvey, "Age, Intelligence and Sex as Variables in the Conformity Behavior of Negro and White Children," *Child Development*, 35: 451–460, 1964.

15. Howard A. Moss, "Sex, Age and State as Determinants of Mother–Infant Interaction," *Merrill-Palmer Quarterly*, 13: 19–36, 1967.

16. See Jerome Kagan and Michael Lewis, "Studies of Attention in the Human Infant," *Merrill-Palmer Quarterly*, 11: 95–127, 1965; Susan Goldberg and Michael Lewis, "Play Behavior in the Year Old Infant: Early Sex Differences," *Child Development*, 40: 21–31, 1969.

17. Jack O. Balswick and Charles W. Peek, "The Inexpressive Male: A Tragedy of American Society," *The Family Coordinator*, 11:363–368, 1971.

18. See, for example, Pauline Bart, "Depression in Middle-aged Women," in Vivian Gornick and Barbara K. Moran (eds.), *Women in Sexist Society*, Basic Books, New York, 1971, pp. 99–117; Robert R. McDonald, "The Role of Emotional Factors in Obstetric Complications: A Review," *Psychosomatic Medi-*

cine, 30: 222–237, 1968; Frederic T. Melges, "Postpartum Psychiatric Syndromes," *ibid.*, pp. 95–108.

19. See William J. Goode, "A Theory of Role Strain," *American Sociological Review*, 25: 483–496, 1960.

20. See William E. Knox and Harriet F. Kupferer, "A Discontinuity in the Socialization of Males in the United States," *Merrill-Palmer Quarterly*, 17: 251–262, 1972.

21. For a discussion of basic conflicts inherent in modern social life as experienced by adolescent males and females, see Chad Gordon, "Social Characteristics of Early Adolescence," *Daedalus*, 10: 931–960, 1971.

22. See Mirra Komarovsky, "Cultural Contradictions and Sex Roles," *American Journal of Sociology*, 52: 182–189, 1946; and Mirra Komarovsky, "Cultural Contradictions and Sex Roles: The Male Case," *American Journal of Sociology*, 78: 873–884, 1973.

23. Matina Horner, *op. cit.*; Rebecca S. Vreeland, "Sex at Harvard," *Sexual Behavior*, 2: 5–10, 1972, and "Is It True What They Say About Harvard Boys?" *Psychology Today*, 5: 65–69, 1972; also, Janet Lever and Pepper Schwartz, *Women at Yale*, Bobbs-Merrill, Indianapolis, Ind., 1971.

24. Lorraine M. Rand and Anna Louise Miller, "A Developmental Cross Section of Women's Career and Marriage Attitudes and Life Plans," *Journal of Vocational Behavior*, 2: 317–331, 1972; Doris R. Entwistle and Ellen Greenberger, "Adolescent's View of Women's Work Role," *American Journal of Orthopsychiatry*, 42: 648–656, 1972.

25. Linda Lytle Holmstrom, *The Two Career Family*, Schenkman, Cambridge, Mass., 1972; J. A. Birnbaum, *Life Patterns, Personality Style and Self-Esteem in Gifted Family-Oriented and Career-Committed Women*. Doctoral dissertation, University of Michigan, Ann Arbor, 1971.

26. Jessie Bernard, *Academic Women*, Pennsylvania State University Press, University Park, 1964, p. 216.

27. The material on sex differences throughout the life cycle must be synthesized from a large variety of sources that are not specifically concerned with this topic. Several excellent and comprehensive sources on life cycle changes are: Lois Wladis Hoffman and Martin L. Hoffman (eds.), *Child Development Research* (2 volumes), Russell Sage Foundation, New York,

1964, 1966; Paul H. Mussen (ed.), *Carmichael's Manual of Child Psychology*, 3rd ed. (2 volumes), Wiley, New York, 1970; Elizabeth Douvan and Joseph Adelson, *The Adolescent Experience*, Wiley, New York, 1966; Matilda White Riley, Ann Foner, and Associates, *Aging and Society* (3 volumes), Russell Sage Foundation, New York, 1968, 1970, 1972; Bernice L. Neugarten (ed.), *Middle Age and Aging*, University of Chicago Press, Chicago, 1968.

28. Neugarten, *ibid.*, p. 71.

29. Alan C. Kerckoff, "Husband–Wife Expectations and Reactions to Retirement," *Journal of Gerontology*, 19: 510–516, 1964; John A. Ballweg, "Resolution of Conjugal Role Adjustment After Retirement," *Journal of Marriage and the Family*, 29: 277–281, 1967.

30. See Irwin Deutscher, "The Quality of Postparental Life," *Journal of Marriage and the Family*, 26: 52–60, 1964; John Clausen, "The Life Course of Individuals," in Riley et al., *op. cit.*, Vol. III, p 489; Mary W. Hicks and Marilyn Platt, "Marital Happiness and Stability: A Review of Research in the Sixties," *Journal of Marriage and the Family*, 32: 553–574, 1970.

31. Jessie Bernard, *The Future of Marriage*, World, New York, 1972, Chapter I.

32. Quoted in Neugarten, *op. cit.*, p. 28.

33. Glenn H. Elder, Jr., "Appearance and Education in Marriage Mobility," *American Sociological Review*, 34: 519–533, 1969.

34. See, for example, Robert R. Bell, "Some Factors Related to the Sexual Satisfaction of the College Educated Wife," *Family Life Coordinator*, 13: 43–47, 1964; Lee Rainwater, "Marital Sexuality in Four Cultures of Poverty," *Journal of Marriage and the Family*, 26: 457–466, 1964; Paul H. Gebhard, "Post-marital Coitus Among Widows and Divorcees," in Paul Bohannan (ed.), *Divorce and After*, Doubleday, Garden City, N. Y., 1970, pp. 81–96; Paul H. Gebhard, "Factors in Marital Orgasm," *Journal of Social Issues*, 22: 88–95, 1966.

35. Robert R. Bell and Jay B. Chaskes, "Premarital Sexual Experience Among Coeds, 1958–1968," *Journal of Marriage and the Family*, 32: 81–84, 1970; Harold T. Christensen and Christina F. Gregg, "Changing Sex Norms in America and Scandinavia," *Journal of Marriage and the Family*, 32: 616–627, 1970, Joel J.

Moss, Frank Apolonio, and Margaret Jensen, "The Premarital Dyad in America During the Sixties," *Journal of Marriage and the Family*, 33: 50–69, 1971; Kenneth L. Cannon and Richard Long, "Premarital Sexual Behavior in the Sixties," *Journal of Marriage and the Family*, 33: 36–49, 1971.

36. See Ira L. Reiss, "How and Why America's Sex Standards are Changing," in John H. Gagnon and William Simon (eds.), *The Sexual Scene*, Transaction Books, Chicago, 1970, pp. 45–57.

37. Ibtihaj Arafat and Betty Yorburg, "On the Pattern of Living Together Without Marriage," *Journal of Sex Research*, 9: 97–106, 1973.

38. John F. Kanter and Melvin Zelnick, "Sexual Experience of Young Unmarried Women in the United States," *Family Planning Perspectives*, 4: 9–17, 1972, and "Contraception and Pregnancy: Experience of Young Unmarried Women in the United States," *Family Planning Perspectives*, 4: 21–35, 1972.

39. See Margaret Clark, "The Anthropology of Aging: A New Area for Studies of Culture and Personality," in Bernice L. Neugarten, *op. cit.*, pp. 433–443.

40. See Arthur B. Shostak and William Gomberg, eds., *Blue Collar World*, Prentice-Hall, Englewood Cliffs, N.J., 1964; Mirra Komarovsky, *Blue Collar Marriage*, Random House, New York, 1964; Irving Tallman and Ramona Marotz, "Life Style Differences Among Urban and Suburban Blue Collar Families," *Social Forces*, 48: 334–348, 1970.

41. Lee Rainwater, Richard P. Coleman, and Gerald Handel, *Working Man's Wife*, Oceana, Chicago, 1959.

42. Melvin L. Kohn, *Class and Conformity*, Dorsey, Homewood, Ill., 1969.

43. John Scanzoni, *Sexual Bargaining*, Prentice-Hall, Englewood Cliffs, N.N., 1972.

44. G. William Domhoff, *The Higher Circles*, Vintage, New York, 1970.

45. See Betty Yorburg, *The Changing Family*, Columbia University Press, 1973, Chapter V.

46. Richard Centers, Bertram H. Raven, and Aroldo Rodrigues, "Conjugal Power Structure: A Re-examination," *American Sociological Review*, 36: 264–277, 1971.

47. John H. Scanzoni, *The Black Family in Modern Society*, Allyn & Bacon, Boston, 1971.

48. For a description of shtetl culture, see Mark Zborowski and Elizabeth Herzog, *Life Is With People*, International Universities Press, New York, 1951.

49. Results of a nationwide survey conducted by the American Jewish Committee and reported in *The New York Times*, February 9, 1973.

50. Centers, Raven, and Rodrigues, *op. cit.*

51. See Harry H. L. Kitano, *Japanese Americans*, Prentice-Hall, Englewood Cliffs, N.J., 1969.

52. Gerald Meredith and Connie Meredith, "Acculturation and Personality Among Japanese College Students in Hawaii," *Journal of Social Psychology*, 62: 175–182, 1966.

53. A comprehensive study of this group, with a good bibliography, is Leo Grebler, Joan W. Moore, and Ralph C. Guzman, *The Mexican American People*, Free Press, New York, 1970.

CHAPTER 6

1. Cited in Ralph Linton (ed.), *Science of Man in the World Crisis*, Columbia University Press, New York, 1945, p. 347.

2. United States Department of Commerce, Bureau of the Census, *Current Population Reports*, 1972.

3. Dean D. Knudson, "The Declining Status of Women: Popular Myths and Failures of Functionalist Thought," *Social Forces*, 48: 183–193, 1969.

4. Inge K. Broverman et al., "Sex Role Stereotypes and Clinical Judgements of Mental Health," *Journal of Consulting Psychology*, 34: 1–7, 1970.

5. John Scanzoni, *Sexual Bargaining: Power Politics in the American Marriage*, Englewood Cliffs, N.J.: Prentice-Hall, 1972.

6. The Virginia Slims' American Women's Opinion Poll, Princeton, N.J., 1971, p. 36.

7. Philip Goldberg, "Are Women Prejudiced Against Women?" *Trans-Action*, 5: 28–30, 1968.

8. See, for esample, Kaoru Yamamoto, Mary Sue Smalling, and Jack Wiersma, "Student Perceptions of Professors in Eight Small Colleges," *Journal of Experimental Education*, 41: 81–90, 1972.

9.   Jessie Bernard, *Academic Women*, Pennsylvania State University Press, University Park, 1964; Helen S. Astin, *The Woman Doctorate in America: Origins, Career, and Family*, Russell Sage Foundation, New York, 1969; Jonathan R. Cole, "American Men and Women of Science." Paper presented at the American Sociological Association Meetings, Denver, Colo., 1971; L. R. Harmon, "High School Ability Patterns: A Look Backward from the Doctorate," Scientific Manpower Bulletin 6, National Research Council, Washington, D.C., 1965.

10. Helen Mayer Hacker, "Women As A Minority Group," *Social Forces*, 30: 60–69, 1951; and "Women As A Minority Group: Twenty Years Later." Unpublished manuscript, 1972.

11. Jessie Bernard, *Women and the Public Interest*, Aldine, Chicago, 1971.

12. Reported in *The New York Times*, April 1, 1973, p. 48. See also, Joseph Bensman, "American Youth and the Class Structure," in Harry Silverstein (ed.), *The Sociology of Youth: Evolution and Revolution*, Macmillan, New York, 1973, pp. 62–82.

13. Reported in *Newsweek*, February 22, 1971, pp. 61–63.

INDEX

215

82, 84, 85, 117, 127, 128,
132–134, 167, 172, 180–181
verbal skills, 15, 28, 158
working class/lower class, 9, 17, 31,
42, 49, 67, 78, 82, 84–85,
87, 161, 168, 169, 176, 179,
180
poor, 31–32, 75, 82, 95, 142–
143
see aslo Children; Economic factors/
employment; Love; Marriage;
Pregnancy and childbirth; and
Women's movement
Freud, Sigmund, 37, 38–39, 41, 43
Fun ethic, 42, 48, 161, 175

Geographic mobility, 68–69, 71, 72,
78, 88, 90, 167, 169, 193
Germany, 149, 150
Germany, East, 150
Germany, West, 117, 150
Government, 10, 12, 32, 68, 93, 96,
98, 102–103, 109–110, 118,
148–152, 188
education, health, and welfare, 32,
97, 103, 118, 193
family allowances and assistance,
12, 30, 32, 66, 97, 193; see
also Children, day care centers
Gratification, 42, 48, 161, 175
sexual, 31–32, 42, 43, 45, 47, 66,
70, 87, 97, 182
Greece (anc.), 73–75
Groups, 3, 7–8, 53, 187–188. See
also Ethnic groups; Women's
movement
Guatemala, 18
Guilt, see Anxiety and guilt

Hacker, Helen, 191
Health, 16, 17, 18, 55, 58, 65, 135,
165, 192, 195
control and cure of disease, 18, 42,
65, 89, 96

government role, 32, 97, 118, 193
middle age, 18, 171, 173, 176
Hinduism, 83, 84, 85
Horney, Karen, 39
Horticultural societies, 39–40, 58–61,
95, 141, 192; see aslo Non-
literate societies
Hunting and gathering societies, 11,
30–31, 54–58, 192; see also
Nonliterate societies

Identity, 1–5, 9
Illegitimacy, 45, 97, 110, 111, 143,
175
Incest taboo, 35–36
Independence, see Dependence/in-
dependence
India (mod.), 18, 83, 85, 86, 91, 105
India (trad.), 83–86
Individualism, 3, 88–89, 90, 151,
154, 161, 167, 179, 194, 195
Industrial revolution, 51–52, 64
Industrial societies, 3, 11, 51, 64–72,
77–78
birthrate, death rate, and life expectancy, 16, 17, 18, 45, 65,
66, 72, 111, 116, 134, 192
divorce, 69, 70, 71
marriage, 32, 48, 61, 66, 69–70,
70–71, 78, 92, 115, 137, 166,
167, 176, 179, 192, 195
mobility (geographic, psychological,
social), 48, 68–69, 71, 72, 78,
85, 88, 90, 91, 167, 169, 174,
186, 193
see also Children; Economic factors/
employment; Education;
Family; Females; Males; Marriage; Science and technology;
Sexual behavior; and individual
countries
Infanticide, female, 18, 80, 82, 103
Infants, see Children
Iran, 138–140
Islam, see Arab countries; Muslims

sexual behavior, 34, 35, 45
see also Horticultural societies;
Hunting and gathering
societies
Nuclear family, 48, 56, 61, 69, 79, 98,
103, 143, 167; *see also*
Geographic mobility

Occupations, *see* Economic factors/
employment
Old age, *see* Aging and old age

Partnership, 69, 70–71, 78, 92, 176,
192, 195; *see also*
Equalitarianism
Passivity, 16, 26
females, 15, 26, 37, 38, 40, 52, 96,
163, 179, 190, 192
see also Fatalism
Patriarchy and patriarchal attitudes,
24, 42, 53, 63, 74, 78, 81,
85–86, 91, 110, 116, 125,
127, 128, 143, 181, 182, 192;
see also Agricultural societies;
Marriage, arranged or controlled
Patrilineal societies, 59, 63
Patrilocal residence, 59, 63, 81, 82
Paul, St., 76
Personality traits, 3–4, 54, 61, 155–
170 *passim*
biological basis, 36–43
see also Individual traits
Polyandry, 60, 85
Polygamy, 62
Polygyny, 59–60, 85, 87, 135, 141,
143, 144–146
Poor, *see* Working class/lower class–
poor
Population, birthrate, 17–18, 65, 72,
87, 117, 134
death rate, 65, 141
size of, and female employment,
105, 110, 117, 118
Portugal, 125, 126
Power, *see* Authority and power

Pregnancy and childbirth, 6, 16, 20,
21, 39, 46, 47–48, 126, 165
barrenness, 65–66, 81
couvade, 39
premarital pregnancy, 96
see also Birth control
Property, 55, 79, 85, 88, 182; *see
also* Marriage, dowry
Psychoanalytic theory, 36–43 *passim*
Psychological mobility, 48, 68–69
Puberty, 20, 36, 45, 60, 84

Rationalism, 88, 89, 90, 128, 130,
151, 179, 183, 194
Recreation, *see* Leisure and recrea-
tion
Religion, 91, 92, 148, 150
agricultural and nonliterate socie-
ties, 58, 60, 62, 64, 73
Hinduism, 83, 84, 85
Islam, 85, 86, 87, 137, 141
Judaism, 183
secularism, rise in, 88, 89, 151, 179
see also Christianity
Renaissance, 77
Role, 3, 4–5, 9
Roman Catholic Church, 125, 126,
128, 130, 150
Romans (anc.), 75–76
Rorschach test, 28, 156
Ross, A. E., 53

Science and technology, 6, 11, 12,
17, 30, 38, 41, 42, 50, 59, 61,
88, 115, 148–152, 193, 194
and health, 18, 42, 65, 89, 96
see also Industrial societies
Secularism, 88, 89, 151, 179
Sex ratio, 17–18
Sex-typed role, 3–4, 9, 10, 153,
154–155; *see also* individual
cultures and societies
Sexual behavior, Africa, sub-Saharan,
141, 142–143
agricultural societies, 31, 63